REPAIR

YOUR OWN

CREDIT

By
Bob Hammond

REPAIR YOUR OWN CREDIT

By
Bob Hammond

CAREER PRESS
180 Fifth Avenue
P.O. Box 34
Hawthorne, NJ 07507
1-800-CAREER-1
201-427-0229 (outside U.S.)
FAX: 201-427-2037

Note: Information given in this book is correct to the best of the authors' knowledge, but its accuracy is not guaranteed. Credit discussions are not meant to be advice, but a starting point for educated decisions.

Repair Your Own Credit
ISBN 1-56414-166-7, $7.99
Cover design by A Good Thing, Inc.
Printed in the U.S.A. by Book-mart Press

To order this title by mail, please include price as noted above, $2.50 handling per order, and $1.00 for each book ordered. Send to: Career Press, Inc., 180 Fifth Ave., P.O. Box 34, Hawthorne, NJ 07507

Or call toll-free 1-800-CAREER-1 (Canada: 201-427-0229) to order using VISA or MasterCard, or for further information on books from Career Press.

Library of Congress Cataloging-in-Publication Data

Hammond, Bob.
    Repair your own credit / by Bob Hammond.
        p.   cm.
    ISBN 1-56414-166-7 : $7.99
    1. Consumer credit—United States. 2. Credit ratings—United
States. I. Title.
HG3756.U54H367   1995
332.7'43—dc20   94-44539
                                                              CIP

ACKNOWLEDGMENTS

There are many people who helped make this book a reality. They include Ron Fry, Larry Wood, Betsy Sheldon and Ellen Scher at Career Press. Also, Peder Lund, Jon Ford, Karen Pochert, Fran Milner, Janice Vierke and Tina Mills at Paladin Press. Excellent books don't happen without excellent publishers.

To Lona Luckett at the Better Business Bureau, Holly Novac at TRW, Russell Deitch at the Federal Trade Commission, Gayle Weller and Susan Henrichsen with the California Attorney General's Office, Nancy Cox with the Riverside County District Attorney's Office, Elliot Blair Smith at the *Orange County Register*, Laurin Jackson at Secretarial Solutions, Lenny Robin of Fresh Start Financial Service, Michael Jay, Michael Hsu, Ken Yarbrough, Greg Sullivan, Stacey Aldstadt, Carmen Vargas, June Lamond, Michael Givel, Dianne Huppman, Executive Director of Consumer Credit Counseling Service of the Inland Empire, Jayson Orvis, Troy Smith, Merrill Chandler of the North American Consumer Alliance and everyone else who made a contribution to this book—thank you.

CONTENTS

C

Repair Your Own Credit

FOREWORD

As director of the Better Business Bureau of the Southland [Southern California], I have witnessed the rise and fall of many scam operations, but few as twisted and far-reaching as the credit repair industry.

The complexity of the system in general has undeniably provided a shield for these fraudulent companies. Advertisements and carefully worded promotional materials put out by these companies led the unsuspecting public to believe that they could somehow magically "fix" or "erase" the negative information in a credit report. This unrealistic idea is indeed appealing to confused, financially strapped families so desperate to regain their purchasing power.

My experience in counseling or assisting victims has shown that most were completely unaware of both the limitations and restrictions that a credit repair firm is subject to and the rights they, as consumers, were entitled to under the Fair Credit Reporting Act.

Once an underground industry, credit repair services eventually came out of the closet with blatant advertising claims. Now, ironically, they are returning to the closet for a time. Tough new consumer protection laws have forced these scam artists to find new ways to disguise their businesses and continue to take advantage of the ignorance of others. There is already evidence that many have resurfaced in the form of financial advisory services, debt consolidators, or even nonprofit organizations. Many key players in the industry have legal backgrounds, which makes it easy for them to utilize loopholes in the laws designed to protect the public from unethical or fraudulent operators. Law enforcement agencies alone cannot combat this problem effectively. Funding is scarce, and the key players in the game know how to use an effectively timed bankruptcy to their advantage.

The answer to this problem: consumer education! I not only consider it my personal responsibility but also the responsibility of all who are educated in this process to spread the word: "You can do it yourself." As an advocate of consumer education and a firm believer that the pen is mightier than the sword, I believe this book can and should be used as an educational weapon.

Thanks, Bob!

Lona J. Luckett
Director of Operations
Better Business Bureau of the Southland

PREFACE

P

Karen Johnson had recently returned from college in Europe and had not yet established credit in the United States. One day she walked into Sam's Auto Mart and picked out a small used car with a sticker price of $9,600. She filled out a credit application, and the salesman left to process it. When the salesman returned, he told Karen he was sorry, but she did not have enough credit to qualify for the loan. Karen went to four other car dealers and got the same reaction. Slick Willie, the salesperson at Too Good Auto Sales, also told Karen that her credit history was insufficient, but added that he could help her establish new credit. Karen, frustrated and in desperate need of a car, decided to go along with Slick Willie's plan.

Slick told Karen that he had a friend who could get her a good credit rating for $900. Slick also promised to reduce the sticker price by that amount. Slick called his friend Felix Fixer and made arrangements for Karen and Felix to meet.

Karen went to Felix's office and wrote him a check for $900. She then went home to wait for Felix to call. Felix went right to work. First he called Blue Sky Bank, a subscriber to a major credit bureau. Felix convinced the clerk at the bank that he was an employee of the credit bureau and that, because of computer problems, he needed to get the bank's credit bureau access code. The clerk responded with the three-digit code.

Next, Felix searched the phone book for other people with the name of Karen Johnson. He used the access code that he obtained from Blue Sky Bank to get credit information from the credit bureau on all of the Karen Johnsons listed in the phone book. When he found a credit report for a Karen Johnson that contained only positive information, he stopped looking. He copied down all of the account information and then contacted Karen and asked her to stop by his office.

When she arrived, Felix gave her the credit information he had obtained and instructed her to use all of the information when filling out an application. He also instructed her to use a mail-drop address that he could control as her current address and to use the "victim's" Social Security number. Karen was now free to apply for credit anywhere.

Karen went back to Too Good Auto Sales and reapplied using this new information. She got the car, Slick and Felix split the $900 and Slick Willie got the commission.

This is just one example of the multitude of credit repair scams that have sprung up around the credit reporting industry, capitalizing on the credit problems of millions of American consumers and exploiting the weaknesses in the credit reporting industry. There are many more.

The flaws that exist in the credit reporting system and the abuses that have occurred in the industry have caused financial injury to a significant number of consumers. However, these flaws and abuses spawned another whole industry—credit repair—which, while perhaps well-intentioned originally, has become riddled with corruption.

Consumers should be wary of credit bureaus and credit repair services alike, because they can be burned by both. The fact is that consumers who wish to have false or inaccurate information removed from their credit reports have little need for credit clinics. Under the rules outlined in the Fair Credit Reporting Act, they can do it themselves easily and inexpensively.

Repair Your Own Credit was written for those consumers who have had credit problems and are considering the services of a credit repair company. It is the first book available on the subject, and it is written by an insider. It is meant to warn consumers of the dangers and pitfalls of credit repair and to empower them to help themselves.

The book is a result of many years of research into the subject of consumer credit, including my own personal experiences as a credit consultant and consumer activist. It is based on firsthand accounts of some of the major players in the credit game and is certain to cause a storm within the industry.

Repair Your Own Credit traces the rise and fall of an industry that was destined to fail. It takes a revealing, if not shocking, look at the scams and scoundrels that gave the credit repair business such a bad reputation and tells how they ended up.

Many of my former associates have cautioned that I may be sacrificing my own livelihood and perhaps even my own freedom and safety by publicizing this book, and perhaps that is so. But, to paraphrase Benjamin Franklin, "Those who would give up essential publicity to purchase a little security deserve neither."

May the eyes of your understanding be enlightened.

THE CREDIT GAME

1

FLASHBACK

For many years, I was engaged in research—studying various strategies for attaining personal and financial freedom. I spent thousands of dollars on books, tapes, newsletters and home-study courses. I attended countless seminars and consulted with numerous self-proclaimed experts on real estate, creative financing, positive thinking, multilevel marketing, mail-order publishing and other plans. Some were very valuable and informative. Others were total ripoffs. I also came across several underground books that claimed to reveal inside secrets and strategies for beating the system. Some of these books contained very interesting and useful information. Others turned out to be not only completely illegal, but frightening as well.

I finally began to get discouraged. None of these plans really seemed to live up to their promises. The only ones who seemed to be getting rich were the promoters themselves. I was tired of being ripped off. I still couldn't help thinking, however, that there must be a way for someone like myself, with an average education and abilities, to get ahead in the world.

Repair Your Own Credit

One day I attended a seminar in Riverside, California, led by an authority on consumer credit. The seminar also featured a former credit bureau executive turned consumer advocate. I listened intently as they took turns explaining credit bureau operations, consumer rights under the Fair Credit Reporting Act, how to have negative information removed from credit files, and the secrets of establishing a new credit identity. The final hour of the seminar was devoted to instructions on setting up a profitable credit consulting firm. I was intrigued by the possibilities. Somehow, this one seemed a little different than the others. Little did I know that it was about to become a major turning point in my life. I left the seminar with an entirely new understanding of the phrase "knowledge is power."

Eagerly, I began the process of clearing up the wreckage of my past and getting my own house in order. My own credit had been devastated by bankruptcy, divorce and many years of reckless living. I was amazed to discover that within a matter of weeks of my applying what I had learned at the seminar, companies that had rejected me previously were suddenly begging me to take their credit cards. I wanted to shout it from the rooftops—"It works! It really works!"

For several years, I worked as a credit consultant with my own company. In working with others, I discovered that most people had information in their credit files that was obsolete, inaccurate or misleading. In many cases, the information belonged to someone else with a similar name. I discovered that people were being discriminated against and turned down for credit, insurance, jobs and even places to live because of the clerical error of some bureaucrat.

During this time, I was involved in a lawsuit against TRW Information Services, one of the largest and most powerful of the consumer credit reporting services or credit bureaus. That prompted me to do some additional research into the way credit bureaus violated the rights of citizens. The culmination of this research was the publication of *How to Beat the Credit Bureaus: The Insider's Guide to Consumer Credit*. This book showed how the credit bureaus were violating the Fair Credit Reporting Act and presented case studies of people who had taken legal action against the bureaus on grounds of defamation, invasion of privacy and negligence.

Consequently, hundreds of lawsuits were filed against the major credit bureaus throughout the country. TRW was among them, with the Federal Trade Commission (FTC) and 19 states filing lawsuits against it. The credit bureaus were forced to make it easier for consumers to obtain information regarding their files and also to dispute erroneous information.

TRW and Equifax awarded thousands of dollars in damages to consumers and agreed to major concessions and policy changes allowing consumers free access to their reports.

With two out of three adult consumers as potential clients, the credit repair industry rose quickly to meet the needs of the millions of individuals with poor credit ratings. Along the way, a parade of con artists, former used car salesmen and self-proclaimed credit gurus took advantage of an opportunity, leaving behind a wake of bare-pocketed consumers. Over the last few years, American consumers have lost more than $50 million collectively by hiring fly-by-night operators to "fix" their credit reports—with few or no results.

Thousands of consumers were complaining of being ripped off by unscrupulous promoters of various credit repair scams. New legislation was passed in an attempt to put a stop to these companies and their deceptive practices. That's when I began writing the book you now have before you. *Repair Your Own Credit* is the first book ever to provide a comprehensive inside look at one of the most controversial of professions.

The following pages provide a shocking inside look at the scams used by credit clinics to bilk millions of dollars from gullible consumers on a daily basis. They also reveal how a group of credit consultants almost brought the credit reporting industry to its knees and how a secret task force was formed to put the scandalous "credit doctors" out of business once and for all.

A Cast Of Characters

2

TRW Information Services

TRW Information Services, based in Orange, California, operates and markets one of the nation's largest computerized consumer credit reporting services, maintaining credit information on more than 180 million consumers in the United States. TRW collects and stores that information and provides it to subscribers that have a "permissible purpose" to use it under the Fair Credit Reporting Act (FCRA). Permissible purposes include granting credit, hiring for employment and underwriting insurance policies. Organizations and companies that subscribe to TRW's service include credit grantors, employers and insurance underwriters.

TRW entered the credit reporting business when it acquired Credit Data Corporation in 1969. This bureau, originally the Detroit-based Michigan Merchants Credit Association, was founded in 1932. In 1960, the company was incorporated in Michigan as Credit Data Corporation and used file cabinets and 3-by-5-inch cards to store consumer credit information. In 1965, Credit Data initiated and installed the first computerized, on-line credit reporting system.

Repair Your Own Credit

For more than two decades, TRW has been the technological leader in the credit reporting industry. It was the first to automate its nationwide database to ensure that consumers' credit histories were kept when they moved or changed their names. In 1989 TRW acquired Chilton Corporation, a major credit reporting company based in Dallas, Texas, to further expand its consumer information services.

In return for the credit information and services offered by TRW, subscribers provide TRW with a record of their past and present credit account information, usually on a monthly basis. This regular receipt of credit information provides TRW with an automatic update of consumer credit account information.

The subscribers' information is typically provided via magnetic tape or cartridge, copied directly from the billing records used to notify their customers. These tapes are sent to TRW's data center in Allen, Texas, where the information undergoes an extensive data-verification process before being entered into the company's computer system. Public record information is gathered directly from court and county records, converted to a computerized format, and entered into the computer system.

TRW uses a search and retrieval system called Accu-Search to find consumers' information in its comprehensive database. TRW's Accu-Search uses four special searches to match consumers' identifying information with their credit history: National, AKA, Nickname, and Expanded Address. Together these searches can check all areas of the country with a single inquiry. Any previous addresses, alternate surnames such as maiden names, and nicknames can be retrieved automatically with the current consumer information.

OTHER CREDIT BUREAUS

TRW is one of three major U.S. computerized credit reporting agencies. The others are Trans Union (based in Chicago) and Equifax, Inc. (headquartered in Atlanta). Another of the nation's larger bureaus, Houston-based Computer Science Corporation (CSC), formerly Associated Credit Services, formed a strategic alliance with Equifax in 1988.

About 900 smaller, independently owned credit bureaus operate nationwide, providing an important service to their communities. TRW has contractual agreements with 55 such bureaus to provide them with the latest data-handling technology and access to its credit reporting services. These agreements allow the bureaus to retain independent control of their operations.

Most credit bureaus are members of Associated Credit Bureaus, Inc., an industry association based in Washington, D.C.

THE BETTER BUSINESS BUREAU

The Better Business Bureau (BBB) was originally founded by Samuel C. Dobbs in 1906 as a vigilance committee to combat unfair advertising practices.

While truth in advertising remains a primary concern for the more than 150 Better Business Bureaus that exist across the country, their mission has expanded to include other programs and goals to make the marketplace a fair and honest place to do business.

Other Better Business Bureau programs and activities include:

- Reporting to inquirers about individual businesses and companies, including information about the company's location, principals, type of business, complaint history and other information to help the caller determine whether he or she wishes to transact business with the company.

- Reporting to inquirers about individual charities to enable the caller to decide whether he or she wishes to contribute.

- Resolving consumer complaints against companies, including mediation and arbitration, when appropriate.

- Setting up long-standing arbitration programs, including one to arbitrate disputes between automobile owners and automobile manufacturers, and another to arbitrate business-consumer disputes involving businesses that have pledged in advance to arbitrate through the Better Business Bureau.

- Cooperating with government authorities in putting fraudulent companies out of business.

- Publishing more than 200 pamphlets and special reports on specific topics of interest to the consuming public.

The BBB considers the credit repair industry to be one of the most problematic in recent years. Many players in the industry have seized the opportunity to take advantage of the poor credit ratings that plague the consuming public. Although there may be legitimate organizations that can help an individual improve or correct credit histories, the industry in general suffers from a well-earned reputation of being a scam. The reason? Unfair and deceptive claims that bad credit can be "erased," or "made extinct." These misrepresentations of services—in advertising and sales pitches—have prompted the Better Business Bureau to wage war on these scam artists through cooperation with law enforcement investigations, advertising challenges, reliability reports to the public, media proposals and, most importantly, consumer education.

THE NATIONAL FOUNDATION FOR CONSUMER CREDIT

The National Foundation for Consumer Credit is a nonprofit membership organization whose goals are to educate, counsel and promote the intelligent use of credit in individual and family financial planning.

As the national organization, NFCC provides leadership for a growing number—now almost 1,000—of nonprofit community Consumer Credit Counseling Services in the United States and Canada.

Consumer Credit Counseling Service (CCCS) provides confidential and professional financial and debt counseling to aid and rehabilitate financially distressed families.

CREDIT REPORTING AGENCIES

3

Across the United States there are several thousand credit bureaus collecting credit information about consumers. These credit bureaus are connected to centralized computer files that contain data on millions of individuals. Almost instantaneously, a credit bureau can produce for a subscribing creditor a revealing report about your past and present credit activity. Although they can operate in different ways, many bureaus follow similar procedures. Banks, finance companies, merchants, credit card companies and other creditors are the paying customers of credit bureaus (subscribers). The subscribers regularly send to credit bureaus reports on their customers containing information about the kind of credit extended, the amount and terms, and paying habits. Some information is collected by the credit bureaus from other sources, such as court records.

WHAT YOUR FILE MAY CONTAIN

The credit bureau file contains your name, address, Social Security number and birth date. A lot of other information also may be included:

- Your employer, position and income.
- Your former address.

- Your former employer.

- Your spouse's name, Social Security number, employer and income.

- An indication that you own your home, rent or board.

And your file may contain detailed credit information. Each time you buy on credit from a reporting store or take out a loan at a bank, finance company or other reporting creditor, a credit bureau is informed of your account number, the date, amount, terms and type of credit. As you make payments, your file is updated to show the outstanding balance, the number of payments and amounts past due, and the frequency of 30-, 60- or 90-day lateness. Your record may indicate the largest amount of credit you have had and the maximum limit permitted by the creditor. Each inquiry about you may be recorded. (If a creditor sees a number of inquiries without credit having been subsequently extended, then he/she may conclude that you have been turned down.) Any suits, judgments or tax liens against you may appear, as well.

THREE MAJOR CREDIT REPORTING AGENCIES

Copy and use the "Credit Report Request" letter (shown in Chapter 13, page 102) to request a copy of your credit report from the credit reporting agencies listed in this section. Be sure to enclose a copy of your driver's license, credit card bill or utility bill. If you have been denied credit within the past 60 days, you can receive a free report from the agency that provided the report. Your request must be accompanied by a copy of the denial letter. TRW will provide a free copy each year regardless of whether you have been turned down for credit.

Note: Each agency may not have the same information, so you may want to obtain a copy of your report from all of them.

TRW Complimentary Report
P.O. Box 2350
Chatsworth, CA 91313-2350
800-392-1122

TRW Credit Data
National Consumer Relations Center
660 N. Central Expwy, Exit 28, P.O. Box 949
Allen, TX 75002
800-682-7654

Use if you need an additional report within the same year and to initiate disputes if you don't have the dispute form that TRW sends with your report. One free copy per year per person. Report fees range from $8 plus sales tax for individuals, unless otherwise stipulated by state law.

Equifax Credit Information Services
P.O. Box 740241
Atlanta, GA 30374-0241
800-685-1111

Report fees are $8 for individuals, unless otherwise stipulated by state law.

Trans Union Credit Information
Consumer Relations Center
P.O. Box 7000
North Olmsted, OH 44070-7000
800-851-2674

Report fees are $8 for individuals, $16 for married couple.

Your Rights Under The Fair Credit Reporting Act

4

Congress enacted the Fair Credit Reporting Act of 1971 to regulate the use of credit reports, require deletion of obsolete information and give the consumer access to his or her file and the right to have erroneous data corrected. A consumer report about you may be issued only to properly identified persons for approved purposes. It may be furnished in response to a court order or in accordance with your own written request; and it may be provided to someone who will use it in connection with evaluation of a credit transaction, employment, underwriting of insurance, determination of eligibility for a license or other benefit granted by a governmental agency or other legitimate business need. Your friends and neighbors who are curious about your affairs may not obtain information about you. To do so might subject the subscriber who obtained it for them to fine and/or imprisonment.

Time Limits On Adverse Data

Most kinds of information in your file may be reported for a period of seven years. If you have declared personal bankruptcy, however, that fact may be reported for 10 years. After seven years or 10 years, the information can't be disclosed by a credit reporting agency unless you are being investigated for a credit application of $50,000 or more, for an application to purchase life insurance of $50,000 or more or for employment at an annual salary of $20,000 or more. In those situations the time limits on releasing the data do not apply. Nor do time limits apply if a creditor chooses to use prior adverse information in his files to deny a new credit relationship.

YOU, TOO, MAY REVIEW YOUR FILE

The Fair Credit Reporting Act gives you the right to know what your credit file contains, and the credit bureau must provide someone to help you interpret the data. You will be required to identify yourself to the bureau's satisfaction, and you may be charged a small fee. There is no fee, however, if you have been turned down for credit, employment or insurance because of information contained in a report within the preceding 30 days (the law may soon allow you 60 days). TRW will provide you with a free copy of your credit report once a year. Trans Union and Equifax will provide you with a free copy of your report if you have been turned down for credit within the last 60 days based on information supplied in their reports. Otherwise the fee is $8 in California.

INCORRECT INFORMATION

Credit bureaus are required to follow reasonable procedures to ensure that subscribing creditors report information accurately. However, mistakes often occur. Your file may contain erroneous data or records of someone with a similar name confused with yours. When you notify the credit bureau that you dispute the accuracy of information, it must reinvestigate and modify or remove inaccurate data. Any pertinent data you have concerning an error should be given to the credit bureau. If reinvestigation does not resolve the dispute to your satisfaction, you may enter a statement of 100 words or less in your file, explaining why you think the record is inaccurate. The law, however, does not require a credit bureau to add to your credit file a statement of circumstances that explains a period of delinquency caused by some unexpected hardship, such as serious illness, a catastrophe or unemployment, which eliminated or drastically reduced your income. This type of explanation should be given by you directly to a credit grantor when applying for credit. The credit bureau must include your statement about disputed data —or a coded version of it—with any reports it issues about you. At your request, the bureau must also send a correction to anyone who received a report in the preceding six months if it was for a credit check, or within a two-year period if it was for employment purposes.

UPDATE TO THE FAIR CREDIT REPORTING ACT

In the summer of 1994, Congress proposed legislation to update The Fair Credit Reporting Act of 1971. Under the proposal (which has not passed as of this writing), bureaus will have to correct errors within 30 days, and will also have to set up toll-free telephone lines and have staff available to answer questions. Businesses that report information to the credit bureaus could face fines for passing on inaccurate information. Here's what it will do when finally signed into law:

- Give you quicker and cheaper access to your credit files. The bill sets a limit of $3 for an annual copy of your credit report from any reporting agency and an $8 charge for additional copies during the course of the year. If you're turned down for a mortgage or other financing because of negative information in your file, credit bureaus will be required to provide you one copy of the report free of charge within 60 days of the "adverse action" by the creditor and at the conclusion of a reinvestigation when incorrect information on you was deleted.

- Provides new protection for consumers disputing information in their files. Credit bureaus will be required to investigate complaints of inaccurate data within 30 days. The bill also requires bureaus to maintain strict procedures to prevent reinsertion of previously deleted, adverse information unless the creditor providing the data can certify its accuracy. In addition, the bill requires consumers to be notified when previously deleted information is put back into their files.

- Places new legal liability on creditors to maintain high standards of accuracy in their own consumer files. For example, if a department store or mortgage lender is notified that its information on you is incorrect, and still does not delete the bad data, you'll be able to sue the creditor for damages.

- Provides new restrictions on lenders and other merchants using your credit files to solicit prequalified borrowers, such as for home equity lines of credit. Also, the bill prohibits the use of a consumer credit report for target marketing without the consumer's express permission and guarantees you the right to have your name removed from future marketing lists.

HIGH-TECH CREDIT RELIEF

In addition to new legislation, technological advances will soon make it easier and faster for consumers to fight credit-report errors and update their report. Until now, consumers who disputed, say, an entry about a credit card account have had to send separate letters to the three national credit bureaus—Equifax, Trans Union and TRW. The bureaus, in turn, would ask the creditor that supplied the questionable data to verify the items, which could take 30 days or more. Now credit bureaus and creditors are plugging into an electronic dispute system that cuts that time to 10 days or less and automatically transmits consumer account changes to all three bureaus. Previously, credit bureaus and creditors mailed paper copies of such data to one another.

CREDIT REPAIR: WHO NEEDS IT?   5

The process of credit reporting begins with the individual consumer. The moment an individual applies for credit, the bureau's monitoring process is initiated. The information supplied in a person's credit application is used to find or establish a file at one or more credit bureaus. This is known as the inquiry process.

HOW CREDIT REPORTING SERVICES WORK

Lending institutions subscribe to credit bureaus in order to obtain the credit and payment history of potential applicants. In turn, some of these subscribers report the payment patterns and credit histories of their own borrowers to the bureaus. Besides creditors such as banks and other financial institutions, retailers, mortgage lenders and oil companies, a bureau's subscribers may include other credit bureaus, insurance companies, collection agencies, employers and professional organizations such as medical and dental groups. Credit bureaus may also supply information to such agencies as the IRS, FBI, welfare departments and local police.

Credit bureaus maintain files on approximately 90 percent of American adult consumers—anybody who ever buys something on credit. Credit grantors, such as banks, department stores and credit card companies, report the payment histories of their customers to one or several credit bureaus.

In less than five years, TRW bought 33 other credit agencies, including the $330 million purchase of Chilton, which added 140 million files to its computers. Equifax put nearly 104 smaller credit bureaus on its network. Trans Union brought aboard 23 agencies and opened offices in 25 new markets. The number of credit bureaus controlled by the "Big Three" collectively doubled during the 1980s to more than 200, giving them data on more than 90 percent of the U.S. adult population.

Each month creditors feed information about your payment history to one or more of the bureaus by computer. The bureaus require companies that request information to supply data on their own customers. Items that end up on your credit file include notices of unpaid bills, court judgments, bankruptcies and property liens.

FLAWS IN THE SYSTEM

For consumers, trying to fix a credit report can be an ordeal. A Santa Ana, California, woman wrote letters and made telephone calls to the Big Three bureaus for six months trying to get another person's bad credit history out of her file. A Chicago man with the same problem couldn't convince a credit bureau there was a mistake, even though the age and addresses of the similarly named man whose information appeared on his report were obviously different from his.

A suburban St. Louis, Missouri, couple had a bankruptcy filing mistakenly placed in their file. Banks then shut off loans to their struggling construction business, forcing them to file bankruptcy for real. They sued but lost.

Credit bureaus enhance the marketability of their reports through the use of internal security systems. Examples include TRW's FACS (File Address Check Service) and CHECKPOINT. Recent consumer complaints indicate that FACS may display messages on a credit report that have adverse connotations. One such message indicated that a consumer was connected in some way with a credit consultant who coincidentally had an office suite in the same high-rise building. In this case, the consumer was a medical doctor who, although qualified for credit in every aspect, was rejected because of the false internal message.

CHECKPOINT may indicate to the user of the credit report that the presence of credit fraud is likely. According to sources at TRW, CHECKPOINT messages appear on more than 90 percent of credit reports reviewed by the consumer relations department. CHECKPOINT messages are often generated as a result of an operator input error. Complaints from consumers have been overwhelming, indicating that many were rejected for credit because of a nonfactual message appearing on their credit reports. These consumers suffered economic injury as a result.

Although the Fair Credit Reporting Act deals specifically with the reporting of adverse information, it does not address the reporting of *positive* information. Negative information is collected by five distinct methods: computerized nine-track tape, manual forms, instant update, inquiry and public record. Positive information is generally obtained by only one method, computerized nine-track tape. Negative information is placed on the credit report for seven years; 10 years in the case of bankruptcy.

Repair Your Own Credit

Positive paid accounts are deleted from the credit report after five years.

According to the Consumer Credit Commission (Commission Update, March 1989), credit bureaus have devised more than 60 categories of reporting credit history, only three of which are of a positive nature. Additionally, credit bureaus are highly selective in their acceptance of information. The business is extremely competitive, and while a customer (subscriber) may report to one credit bureau, chances are that the same subscriber will not report to others. Since smaller companies often simply do not have the opportunity to report either positive or negative history, the creditor is deprived of information that might otherwise have been a decisive factor in the credit-granting decision. Consumers have expressed concern that the partial reporting of credit information does not accurately reflect their creditworthiness.

WHY THE NEED FOR CREDIT DOCTORS?

The booming credit repair business is a recent phenomenon. According to Dr. Bill Tener, director of Regulatory Compliance at TRW Information Services, 10 percent of TRW's computerized credit files contained negative information in 1967. Today, (according to Greg Henchey, TRW's facilitator for its "Focus on Fraud" seminar) that figure is closer to 70 percent.

In determining whether to grant or deny credit, credit grantors use the five "Cs": character, capacity, capital, collateral and conditions. The major credit bureaus have developed an elaborate system by which to identify the "character" of a consumer. The system looks at the individual's credit report and, more specifically, his or her bill-paying habits. The Consumer Credit Commission estimates that approximately 200 million such credit reports are generated and sold annually.

The credit report contains items of personal identification, credit bureau notations, credit history, public record information and a list of persons who have reviewed its contents over the past two years. The report retails for approximately $2 and is received at the user's location through a computer modem.

Credit reporting dates back more than 50 years to the advent of manual reporting agencies. Computerized credit reporting began in the mid-1960s and has evolved into an extremely profitable business today. Trade secrets and proprietary information are safeguarded and released only to those who have a "need" to know. For that reason, it is nearly impossible to find one individual within a credit bureau who is aware of all aspects of credit reporting. Credit bureaus have compartmentalized each of their operational and marketing functions so that individual employees know only one small aspect of the business. Moreover, specific structures of power and influence within each department further promote this environment of secrecy. The public affairs and legislative affairs departments are used to convey information to the public and legislative and enforcement bodies. No matter how well-intentioned the managers of either of these departments may be, they merely parrot information that has been carefully guided through the corporate political maze.

Congress enacted the Fair Credit Reporting Act as a means of protecting consumer rights. It was not intended to give specific authority for credit bureaus to operate a profit-making enterprise. However, the Fair Credit Reporting Act is precisely what credit bureaus quote most often in an attempt to legitimize questioned actions. For instance, Section 609 states, "Every consumer reporting agency shall upon request and proper identification of any consumer, clearly and accurately disclose to the consumer: (3) The recipients of any consumer report on the consumer which it has furnished for (A) employment purposes within the two-year period preceding the request, and (B) for any other purpose within the six-month period preceding the request."

The inquiry process is the means by which credit bureaus choose to conform to the above section. By policy, the inquiry remains on the file for a period of two years. Through workshops and publications, credit bureaus have taught subscribers to view too many inquiries as a danger sign. As a result, having more than two inquiries is usually cause for application rejection on a point score system.

Many consumers have complained that no specific authorization was made to generate an inquiry into their credit records; however, credit bureaus have in most cases declined to remove any and all inquiries through the dispute process as described in Section 611 of the FCRA. Moreover, consumers who have complained to the credit bureaus have received form letters indicating their disputes will not be investigated.

Investigations by the Consumer Credit Commission have shown that these consumers applied for a credit card with a major oil company, which generated an inquiry and evaluated the credit report and later generated a series of four additional inquiries to prevent the subsequent issuance of credit cards by competitors. The consumers complained to the credit bureau and were given a response indicating that inquiries must remain in their files for two years by law and nothing could be done to eliminate this requirement.

Section 60S of the FCRA states,

> *No consumer reporting agency may make any consumer report containing any of the following items of information:*
>
> (1) *Cases under Title 11 of the United States Code or under the Bankruptcy Act that, from the date of entry of the order for relief or the date of adjudication, as the case may be, antedate the report by more than 20 years.*
>
> (2) *Suits and judgments which, from date of entry, antedate the report by more than seven years or until the governing statute of limitations has expired, whichever is the longer period.*
>
> (3) *Paid tax liens which, from date of payment, antedate the report by more than seven years.*
>
> (4) *Accounts placed for collection or charged to profit and loss which antedate the report by more than seven years.*
>
> (5) *Records of arrest, indictment, or conviction of crime which, from date of disposition, release, or parole, antedate the report by more than seven years.*
>
> (6) *Any other adverse item of information which antedates the report by more than seven years.*

Specifically, the law requires that "no" report shall be made containing any of the foregoing; however, credit bureaus repeatedly state to consumers that, according to the FCRA, negative information "must" be reported for seven years or, if it is bankruptcy related, 10 years.

Section 611 states,

If the completeness or accuracy of any item of information contained in his file is disputed by the consumer, and such dispute is directly conveyed to the consumer reporting agency by the consumer, the consumer reporting agency shall, within a reasonable period of time, reinvestigate and record the current status of that information unless it has reasonable grounds to believe that the dispute by the consumer is frivolous or irrelevant. If after such reinvestigation such information is found to be inaccurate or can no longer be verified, the consumer reporting agency shall promptly delete such information.

THE BUREAUS FIGHT BACK

Recently, TRW generated thousands of form letters and sent them to consumers who disputed information on their credit files. The letter informed these consumers that their disputes were determined to be frivolous and irrelevant and thus would not be reinvestigated.

The phrase "frivolous and irrelevant" is somewhat ambiguous and needs appropriate clarification. Certainly, the wording of a dispute could lead a credit bureau to believe it is frivolous and irrelevant. For instance, such a dispute might read, "I was 60 days delinquent in making a payment because I was in the hospital and could not make the payments." This statement is perhaps true and indeed unfortunate; however, the bureau considers it frivolous and irrelevant because it merely confirms the information on the report and does not challenge fact.

According to the Federal Trade Commission, disputes that call for action should not be considered frivolous and irrelevant. An example might be, "I was never late in making my payments; you have me confused with someone else. Please reinvestigate this matter."

Allegations against consumers and credit repair companies have centered around the untruthfulness of disputes. Credit bureaus claim the majority of disputes received are deceptive. The legal "test" falls under the heading of "good faith belief." Good faith belief is determined through the use of the consumer's good memory and substantiating records.

How The Credit Repair Industry Earned A Bad Name

According to the Consumer Credit Commission, some credit repair organizations have instructed their clients to violate the "good faith belief" and dispute entirely accurate information in hopes of achieving deletion. Credit repair organizations that use this particular practice injure the consumer, credit bureau and credit grantor. Credit repair involves the marketing of services to consumers whose credit bureau reports contain negative information that interferes with their ability to obtain credit. The principal method employed by a vast majority of credit repair organizations to improve consumers' credit reports is the dispute procedure available to consumers under Section 611 of the FCRA. This section is designed to provide consumers with a self-help mechanism to correct credit reports that contain inaccurate or incomplete information. Correcting and updating such information ᴜ.....ᴇfits creditors as well as consumers by helping to ensure that credit-granting decisions are made on the basis of complete and accurate information reflecting the consumer's probable creditworthiness.

Many consumers who turn to credit repair firms for help have experienced significant credit problems in the past, which they hope to minimize. In the event that the negative information reported about them is accurate and verifiable, FCRA dispute procedures are unlikely to be of help. Nonetheless, through advertisement and oral representations, credit repair organizations often lead consumers to believe that adverse information in their credit reports can be deleted or modified regardless of its accuracy. Their services are frequently sold on a money-back-guarantee basis, but consumers have reported difficulties in obtaining refunds. The company may be out of business, lack the funds to pay by the time consumers seek refunds, or simply refuse to honor its guarantee. Credit repair organizations have caused economic injury to credit bureaus as well as to consumers in this regard.

Associated Credit Bureaus has published, in concert with the Federal Trade Commission, a consumer guide that reads, "Neither you nor anyone else can require a credit bureau to delete accurate information." The Fair Credit Reporting Act specifically states that disputed information must be deleted if it meets any of three criteria: First, if it is inaccurate; secondly, if it can no longer be verified; and finally, if it is obsolete. So, in addition to requiring that inaccurate information be removed, the law requires the deletion of disputed information that can no longer be verified or is found to be obsolete.

This is important to note, because experience has shown that some credit grantors do not verify information more than 25 months old. The reason for this is that the

Equal Credit Opportunity Act requires creditors to maintain written documentation for a minimum of 25 months. Some time after that period, creditors purge the information. Thus, disputed information is, in fact, frequently deleted from the credit report because it truly can no longer be verified.

Credit bureaus are required by Section 611 of the FCRA to reinvestigate disputed information within a reasonable period of time and to delete information that they cannot verify. A credit bureau may delete accurate information from a consumer's credit bureau report because it is overwhelmed by disputes generated by credit repair organizations or because creditors fail to respond promptly to verification requests.

In the past, certain credit repair firms have attempted to deluge credit bureaus with numerous sequential disputes. They would send the identical dispute to the credit bureau six times—once every three days. The credit bureaus were not set up to handle such a strategy but attempted to do so using outdated procedures.

When a dispute was received, it would be given to one of 50 consumer relations clerks, who would in turn generate a consumer dispute verification form. The form was then submitted to the source of the information for a reply. Three days later an identical dispute would arrive, and the same process would be followed. The credit repair companies alleged that the disputes were not being returned to the credit bureau because the creditor (source) was confused. Perhaps he had returned one dispute form but not another, and as a result, the information was purged from the files.

The bureaus used two avenues to combat this situation. The first involved placing a coded message on the credit report, which, for a period of 30 calendar days, depicted the identification and relationship of the consumer with a particular consumer relations clerk, thereby avoiding subsequent frivolous or irrelevant disputes. Avenue number two involved the deletion of information that was not returned from the source within 20 working days; however, if it was later returned, it was added to the file and treated as new information. This procedure appears to have been effective in combating such strategies used by credit repair companies.

BUILDING A BETTER MOUSETRAP

According to Ken Yarbrough, executive director of the Consumer Credit Commission, a more practical approach to the current credit problems experienced in this country would comprise the following:

1. Creation of a consumer reporting agency that integrates and fully verifies information received from credit bureaus, credit grantors and the consumer to whom it relates, and provides a certified consumer report.

2. Education of credit grantors relating to creditworthiness and interpretations of consumer reports.

3. Provision of detailed educational programs concerning consumer budgeting procedures; long-term, intermediate and immediate financial goals; and consumer credit rights.

4. Production of a detailed consumer financial plan to include a strategy for savings, investments and charity, as well as a strategy for the acquisition of major purchases that must be financed, such as automobiles, real estate, etc.

THE LAW AND THE CREDIT CONSULTANT

6

There are a number of federal laws that affect consumer credit information. The Fair Credit Reporting Act, Equal Credit Opportunity Act and Fair Credit Billing Act, enforced by the Federal Trade Commission, are the three most important.

FAIR CREDIT REPORTING ACT

This act, effective since 1971, gives consumers the following rights:

- To know what credit information is held that relates to them, without charge, if they've been denied credit based on a credit report within 30 days (industry practice is to extend this to 60 days).

- To know who has received a report about them in the past six months and who has received a report for employment purposes within the past two years.

- To have information pertaining to them that they dispute reverified and corrected or removed if inaccurate or unverifiable and to have an updated report sent to those credit grantors who have received a report about them in the last six months.

- To place a statement in the credit reporting company's records if they continue to dispute the accuracy of an item after reverification.

- Not to have adverse information kept or reported for more than seven years, or up to 10 years for bankruptcies.

EQUAL CREDIT OPPORTUNITY ACT

Effective since 1975, this law gives consumers the following rights:

- To be judged on an equal basis with all other credit applicants.

- To have joint accounts reported for both spouses separately after June 1977.

- To have income considered without regard to sex or marital status.

- To have regularly received child support and alimony payments counted as income, if requested.

- Not to be asked questions about birth control or childbearing plans.

- To obtain credit cards in their own names if they are married women.

- To know the reasons they have been denied credit.

FAIR CREDIT BILLING ACT

This act, in effect since 1975, gives consumers the following rights:

- To file a written complaint with the credit grantor within 60 days of the bill they question being mailed to them.

- To receive an acknowledgment from that credit grantor within 30 days of filing the complaint and a settlement within 90 days.

- To forestall collection of the account until the dispute is resolved.

- To prohibit that credit grantor from reporting negative information regarding the disputed amount to the credit reporting agencies until the dispute process is completed.

CALIFORNIA CREDIT SERVICES ACT OF 1984

In the prophetic year of 1984, TRW successfully lobbied for a California law requiring credit service companies to adhere to a strict set of bonding requirements and regulatory restrictions. This law was known as the Credit Services Act of 1984. Similar laws have been enacted in a majority of states.

The stated purposes of the act are to provide prospective clients of credit services organizations with the information necessary to make intelligent decisions regarding the purchase of those services and to protect the public from unfair or deceptive advertising and business practices.

The truth, however, is that the act was intentionally designed to put the credit repair companies out of business—once and for all. Conversations with a number of consultants revealed that the common opinion is that the bonding and contractual requirements place an undue hardship upon the consultant's ability to function effectively for the client. Many are even of the opinion that the act is unconstitutional in that it places severe restrictions upon the free speech of individuals. As a result, many of the credit repair agencies have either simply ignored this law completely or have gone underground by incorporating their credit consulting into another form of business, such as real estate, financial planning or auto brokering. Others have simply ceased advertising and have relied on word of mouth to generate new clientele.

According to the Credit Services Act of 1984, a credit services organization is anyone who provides any of the following services:

1. Improving a buyer's credit record, history or rating.

2. Obtaining an extension of credit for a buyer.

3. Providing advice or assistance to a buyer regarding the above.

These regulations do not apply to:

- Regulated financial institutions (e.g., mortgage or loan companies).

- Banks and savings and loan associations whose accounts or deposits are eligible for federal deposit insurance.

- Licensed prorators (people who, for a fee, receive money from debtors and distribute the money in payment to the debtors' creditors).

- Real estate brokers licensed by the California Department of Real Estate.

- Attorneys.

- Brokers or dealers registered with the Securities and Exchange Commission or the Commodity Futures Trading Commission.

The credit services agency must provide the consumer with a written contract that contains the following:

- A complete description of the services to be performed.

- Any guarantees or promises about refunds.

- The date by which the services will be performed.

- The agency's name, principal business address and the name of a responsible representative of the agency.

- All terms and conditions of payment.

- A disclosure statement describing the consumer's right to cancel the contract within five days for any reason. The contract must be accompanied by a "Notice of Cancellation" form detailing the five-day cancellation rights and must contain a blank cancellation form.

The credit services agency must also provide the consumer with a written description containing the following:

- Information about the agency's trust account or bond.

- Complete information about the consumers' legal rights to review their credit record and to dispute the accuracy of items in the report.

- The approximate price that will be charged for a credit report.

If a consumer cancels the contract, the agency must return the deposit within 15 days of the date of cancellation.

Credit service agencies must also obtain a surety bond or establish a trust account of $5,000, or 5 percent of the total amount of fees charged during the previous 12 months (to a maximum of $25,000). If a credit services agency fails to provide the promised services, these funds will be used to reimburse the consumer.

It is illegal for an agency to charge money for referrals to retail sellers to which a person could apply directly for credit. Also, agencies may not make untrue or misleading statements to any credit reporting bureau or agency about an individual's credit standing or capacity, or advise an individual to make such statements.

Violation of any of these provisions is a misdemeanor, punishable under local and state laws. The agency is also vulnerable to lawsuits in small claims court or municipal court, depending upon the amount of monetary damages claimed. A consumer who files suit against a credit service agency can claim damages plus attorney's fees and costs.

In January 1993, the Credit Services Act (California) was amended to include the following provisions.

Every credit services organization must:

1. File a registration application with, and receive a certificate of registration from, the attorney general's office before doing business in California.

2. Obtain a $100,000 surety bond from an admitted surety in favor of the State of

California for the benefit of any person damaged by any violation of the Act (which must be maintained for two years after the credit services organization stops doing business in California).

3. Give the buyer, before the contract for services is signed, an information statement that contains: (a) a complete and detailed description of the services to be provided and the total cost or obligation to the buyer; (b) notice of the buyer's right to bring legal proceedings against the company's bond and the name and address of the surety which issued the bond; (c) a complete and accurate statement of availability of non-profit credit counseling services; and (d) a statement of consumers' rights under the state and federal credit reporting laws to obtain their credit reports and to dispute inaccurate information in them.

4. Not provide any service to a buyer except pursuant to a written contract which includes a "Notice of Cancellation."

5. Complete the agreed services within 90 days of the date the buyer signs the contract for services.

6. Maintain an agent for service of process in this state (California).

Because the new law exempts "nonprofit" corporations, many credit repair companies are applying to the IRS for tax-exempt status. Some are offering senior citizen discounts and consumer education in order to qualify.

Repair Your Own Credit

According to California State Deputy Attorney General Susan Henrichsen, Ontario-based Coast Credit is the only company to register with the Department of Justice and put up the bond. She said an application from a second company is pending. Some companies are ignoring the law completely. In other cases, companies have folded but employees have gone to work for lawyers, who are exempt from the new law under certain circumstances. While some companies are maneuvering around the law, several are challenging its constitutionality in federal court. The companies argue the bonding requirement will force them out of business.

The companies' request to suspend enforcement of the law until the case is settled next year was denied by the lower court.

CREDIT REPAIR SCAMS AND OTHER TRICKS OF THE TRADE

7

"Got bad credit? Bankruptcy, foreclosures, repossessions? No problem," declare newspaper and television ads promising to fix your credit record or get you credit cards and car loans.

With millions of consumers struggling to overcome spotty credit histories, hundreds of companies have sprung up to take advantage of their predicament. Many of them, according to law enforcement agencies and the Better Business Bureau, are ripoffs.

The bottom line on credit repair, according to the nonprofit National Foundation for Consumer Credit in Silver Spring, Maryland, is that private companies cannot do anything you cannot do yourself.

Under the Federal Fair Credit Reporting Act, credit bureaus must tell individuals who ask what their credit files show. If the information is inaccurate, the consumer can challenge it free of charge. The credit bureau has 30 days to confirm the data or remove it from the file.

But if legal judgments, bankruptcies or other pieces of your credit history are valid, nothing can change them.

Many consumers who have paid for credit repair services have ended up with worse credit than they had before.

Repair Your Own Credit

According to an article in the *Riverside Press Enterprise* (May 20, 1991), Etta Grant, a Mineral Springs, North Carolina, hairdresser, met with a Charlotte salesman for Nationwide Credit Corporation and agreed to pay $1,197 for services. In fall 1989, she put $200 down and wrote six $166.17 postdated checks to be cashed once a month.

Nationwide cashed three of the postdated checks, then deposited the fourth one early. There wasn't enough money in Grant's account yet to cover it, so her credit record actually got worse when it and other checks she had written bounced, according to the summary. The attorney general's office and Grant's private attorney haven't been able to get a refund from Nationwide, which is based in Memphis.

Including Grant's case, the North Carolina Attorney General's Office is investigating 15 complaints against Nationwide Credit and two other companies at Nationwide's Tennessee address. The companies also have been under investigation by Tennessee authorities and the Federal Trade Commission. The FTC wouldn't comment on its findings, and the Tennessee investigation is continuing.

A patchwork of state laws make controlling credit repair firms difficult. And while the three Nationwide companies are headquartered in Memphis, said consumer-protection specialist Phyllis Kitten of the Tennessee Attorney General's Office, "They kept saying they don't do business in Tennessee. And they say they don't do credit repair."

According to the National Center for Financial Education, consumers nationwide and U.S. servicemen overseas lost more than $50 million collectively from 1989 to 1993 as a result of hiring fly-by-night operators to "fix" personal credit files, with little or no results.

A typical scenario is as follows:

> *XYZ Company comes into town and launches a major advertising campaign. They claim that they will remove everything from your credit report for $500. Within 30 days they have enrolled 1,000 people and skipped town—to the tune of a cool half-million. Not bad for a month's work and a little advertising.*

Many such scams have been perpetrated by rings of proficient con men. More often, however, the credit consultant begins with perfectly good intentions. What happens is usually something like this:

> *Bill Mooch spends his late nights watching cable TV shows about how to get into real estate with no money down or borrow millions of dollars on your credit cards. One night he sees a program about the dynamic opportunity in credit consulting. He calls the toll-free number, pays his $129, breezes through the course, and becomes a "professional credit consultant"—certificate and everything.*
>
> *After that he sends in more money to become an associate. For only $1,000 more, he gets a briefcase and a set of business cards. Now he's really in business. He begins a massive advertising campaign. The credit cards are now at the limit. Then it happens. Money starts pouring in. He's got more business than he can handle. "Honey, what did you do with the Johnson file?"*
>
> *Not to worry, though. He'll find the file later. Right now there are more important things to do—like sign up more clients. At $500 to $1,000 per client, Bill is on a serious roll.*

Three months later the phone calls from the first clients start coming in: "I haven't heard anything on my case. My credit is still messed up! I want my money back."

Bill freaks out. "Honey, have you seen the Johnson file?" A week later, Bill and his wife decide to take a vacation—a permanent one. "What the heck, we can afford it," they decide.

A credit consultant in Orange County, California, made a fortune by obtaining credit card applications from creditworthy individuals for a fee. Here's how it worked. The consultant would go to firms who wanted to get creditworthy individuals to accept their credit cards. He made deals with oil companies, department stores, banks, rent-a-car firms and many others, to pay so much for each valid credit application he turned in.

To put this on a wholesale plan where he could reap $20 or more per application, he went to the county records office and got the names and the mortgage holders of homeowners in the area. He would then call the homeowners, identifying himself as representing the mortgage holder on the property and state that he needed a credit update. He would proceed to get all the information on a current application form and inquire as to which credit cards the people already held. All the companies he was representing whose credit cards the consumers *didn't* already have received these filled-out forms as applications for credit cards. He informed the people that he had made arrangements with some companies to issue credit cards to them, that there was no obligation on their part to use them, but that they could come in handy in emergencies. Most people were amenable to this and raised no fuss. The consultant grossed well over $100,000 in a period of four weeks.

Another scam works like this:

A credit repair company obtained a listing of recent bankruptcy filings from the public records. The company sent out letters to the recent filers full of dire warnings about their inability to get any kind of credit, perhaps for as long as 10 years—no credit cards, car loans, personal loans or mortgages.

However, for a fee, the credit repair company promised to help by providing instructions on how to create a new credit identity. After paying the fee, the consumers received instructions on applying for an Employer Identification Number (EIN) from the Internal Revenue Service. The credit repair company advised them to use the employer ID in place of their Social Security numbers when applying for credit. It also advised them to use a new mailing address (usually that of a relative or friend).

Later, when a bank or department store ran a credit check on the alias, it turned up nothing, especially if the name had been changed. That is because the credit bureaus have no way of linking a fake ID with the real individual using it.

The credit bureaus believe that numerous alternate credit identities have slipped onto their data bases, which contain more than 200 million names.

They have taken steps to further protect their systems from fraud. But according to Barry Connelly, vice president of Associated Credit Bureaus, Inc., "It's not fail-safe."

Credit One Services of Ft. Bragg, California, is the largest such operation uncovered so far. Before being shut down in April 1992, with the arrest of its owner, John P. Ruggeri, and his wife, Nancy, Credit One had sold its $39 kits to 20,000 people.

In March 1992, the IRS put out an alert on Credit One, warning that anyone who got involved in the scheme could face tax fraud charges. The agency had noticed a rise in mismatched Social Security numbers that it could not explain. At the same time, the Better Business Bureau alerted the IRS to complaints about Credit One. The Los Angeles City Attorney's Office filed criminal charges, while the FTC, the State Department of Consumer Affairs and the Attorney General's Office filed civil lawsuits seeking fines. The U.S. Postal Service seized the Ruggeris' mail, and the FTC froze their bank accounts.

John and Nancy Ruggeri pleaded no contest to criminal violations of the state's credit repair laws and business code. Nancy Ruggeri was sentenced to 30 days in jail and 30 days under house arrest. John Ruggeri was sentenced to five months in the Los Angeles County jail. The couple contend that their First Amendment rights have been violated and are seeking to set aside their criminal records.

In 1993, Ramlan Press, a company based in Scottsdale, Arizona, began offering a similar program called "Get Credit Now." In addition to encouraging consumers to illegally use the EIN, the manual also plagiarized my book *Credit Secrets: How to Erase Bad Credit*.

The Federal Trade Commission recently published a bulletin warning consumers to be on the alert for unscrupulous credit repair companies that offer to create a new credit file by instructing individuals to obtain an EIN from the IRS. An EIN, which resembles a Social Security number, is used by businesses for reporting financial information to the IRS and the Social Security Administration. The bulletin states that these credit repair companies are instructing individuals with bad credit to use the EINs in place of their Social Security numbers, along with a new mailing address.

The following are instructions from one such credit repair company on establishing a new credit identity:

> *"To establish a new credit file, you apply with the Internal Revenue Service for a Taxpayer's Identification Number (also called an EIN). The required form is an SS4 Form, which can be obtained by calling the IRS at 800-829-1040 and providing your mailing address. To avoid confusion, you need not explain to the IRS representative why you are requesting the form. (The form has many other uses, including being required for any new business.)*
>
> *"Please follow the instructions listed below exactly.*
>
> *1. Print your name on Line 1.*
>
> *2. Go to Line 4a and print your current residence address.*
>
> *3. Print your city, state and zip code on Line 4b. Skip to Line 8a. Check the first box labeled "Individual" and write your Social Security number on the line to the right.*
>
> *4. Go to Line 9 and check the box labeled "Banking purpose" and write "loan" after the arrow to the right.*
>
> *5. Skip Lines 10 through 17c.*

6. *Print your name in the area indicated at the bottom of the form.*

7. *Sign and date the form where indicated.*

"(If you currently have an EIN for business, you can still be issued another number for "banking and loan purposes." There is no need to complete the information on Line 17a, b, and c.)

"You then return the form to the IRS by mail. The correct address for you to mail the form to is shown on the Instruction Sheet, which comes with the SS-4 Form. We do not recommend applying for your number by telephone as offered in the instructions. Instead, you should just mail your completed form to the IRS Center which services your area. In about three to four weeks, you should receive your Taxpayer's ID number by mail. This number is similar to a Social Security number for identification purposes and has the same number of digits, although you'll need to write it in the familiar three-digit, two-digit, four-digit format used in Social Security numbers.

*"After you have obtained your Taxpayer's ID number, you will then need to obtain a new mailing address for credit that is different from where you now live. **Do not use any previous address you have used for credit in the past.** Choose a friend or relative that lives in a different zip code, even if it's just one digit that's different. On any new credit applications, simply list this new address as your current residence address.*

"You will use your new address and Taxpayer's ID number on all credit applications you submit. You must never use your Social Security number or

previous addresses on any credit application as this will cause your new credit file to become connected to your old credit file. It is, however, okay to list your current employer's name and address. This is usually required for any credit approval anyway and normally will not cause a connection with your old credit report.

"Your Social Security number should be used on all Social Security documents; your new Taxpayer's ID number should be used on everything else, including your W2 form and for the payment of taxes. You can even have your employer change your records by completing a new W4 form with your new ID number. This will allow you to have paycheck stubs and income tax forms, which are sometimes required by creditors, that match your new Taxpayer's ID number.

"It is also suggested that you change the address shown on your driver's license to your new address. This is for the times when you are applying for credit and asked to show a photo ID, such as, when you are opening a new bank account. If your state requires that your license show your Social Security number, then try to obtain a new license with your new Taxpayer's ID number as well as your new address.

"To establish a new credit file, simply apply for credit using your Taxpayer's ID number in place of your Social Security number and your new mailing address in place of your current address. Usually, the creditor will have the credit bureau run a 'credit check' on you using the information you provide on your application. (We recommend that this first application for credit be a 'mail-in' type of application as opposed to a 'face-to-face interview' type of application.)

Repair Your Own Credit

"Normally, you will be declined for credit on this first application because of 'no credit history' or 'credit too new to rate.' However, by applying for credit with your new ID number and address, you literally 'force' the computers at the credit bureau into creating a new credit file, containing the new information from your application and showing only the one 'inquiry.' (This occurs due to the fact that their computer database search cannot bring up an existing credit file 'match.')

*"In beginning your new credit, there are several things you must **not do:***

1. ***Do not** apply for credit at any bank, finance company or store that you have previously had credit with.*

2. ***Do not** open a new checking account at a bank that you have had any account with in the past.*

3. ***Do not** list any previous creditors that you have had an account with under your Social Security Number when filling out any new credit application.*

4. ***Do not** list any of your previous addresses on any new credit application.*

5. ***Do not** attempt to add favorable credit references from creditors that appear on your old credit reports."*

According to IRS spokesman Larry Wright, people who change their Social Security numbers as the kits instruct are cheating themselves of future Social Security payments for the years they work. Of more immediate concern, he said, is that the victims of the fraud could be criminally liable for falsifying tax records. He said the promoters of the scheme could be liable for participating in a conspiracy to defraud the government.

Here's what the FTC says: "It is a federal crime to make any false statements on a loan or credit application, which the credit repair company may advise you to do. It is a federal crime to misrepresent your Social Security number. It is also a federal crime to obtain an EIN from the IRS under false pretenses."

As if that weren't enough, the commission also warns that you could be charged with mail or wire fraud if you use the mail or telephone to apply for credit and provide false information. And you may be guilty of civil fraud under many state laws.

In a variation of this scam, the operator of a credit repair company in Los Angeles would assist his "clients" in establishing new credit files by transposing numbers of their Social Security numbers and changing their names and addresses. The clients would be instructed in how to obtain numerous credit cards with high credit limits. Working together, the operator and his clients would obtain large cash advances and make numerous credit purchases until all of the credit limits were exceeded. The clients would then file bankruptcy, wipe out the debts and reestablish credit under a new file. The scam would then be repeated over and over with various accomplices.

ADVANCE-FEE LOAN SCAMS

Beware of advertisements for "advance-fee" or "guaranteed" consumer and small business loans. The FTC is investigating complaints about companies that guarantee loans for financially strapped consumers and small business owners.

Repair Your Own Credit

Advertisements that promise loans generally appear in the classified sections of local and national newspapers, magazines and tabloids. They also may appear in mailings, radio spots and on local cable channels. Often 900 numbers that result in charges on your phone bill or toll-free 800 numbers are featured in the ads. These companies also prefer to use delivery systems other than the U.S. Postal Service, such as overnight or courier services, to avoid detection and prosecution by postal authorities.

Some companies claim they can guarantee you a loan for a fee paid in advance. The fee may range from $100 to several hundred dollars. Small businesses have been charged as much as several thousand dollars as an advance fee for a loan.

Legitimate credit grantors may charge fees to process your loan application, but they will not guarantee that you will qualify for a loan. Illicit advance-fee loan schemes, on the other hand, either promise or strongly suggest that a loan will be provided in exchange for an up-front fee. Salespeople for such companies also may verbally promise that some or all of your advance fee will be refunded if your application is unsuccessful. Some fraudulent companies also may claim that your advance fee will be credited toward repayment of the loan. Usually none of these claims is true.

The FTC suggests taking the following precautions before responding to ads for advance-fee loans:

- Be wary of advertising claiming bad credit is not a problem in securing a loan. If money is not available to you through traditional lending institutions, it is unlikely to become available in response to a classified ad.

- Be cautious of lenders who use toll-free and 900 numbers. You may call a toll-free number which then directs you to dial a 900 number. You pay for 900-number calls, of course, and the charges may be high.

- Check out the company. Contact your local consumer protection agency and the state attorney general's office to learn if they have received any complaints about companies offering advance-fee loans. Keep in mind, however, that suspect companies often establish their operations in one state, advertise heavily for only a few months, collect their loan fees, only to close up shop and move on to another state before complaints are registered and local authorities have a chance to act. Therefore, just because your local consumer protection agency has no complaints on file does not mean that an advance-fee loan business is legitimate.

Be careful about making any loan agreements over the phone. Do not give your credit card, checking account or Social Security numbers over the phone unless you are familiar with the company. This information can be used against you with other frauds. For example, if you give your checking account number over the phone to a stranger for "verification" or "computer purposes," the number may be used to debit (withdraw) money from your checking account.

Ask to review any company's offer in writing, and make sure you understand the terms of the agreement before you complete the transaction.

REQUESTING YOUR CREDIT REPORT, STEP BY STEP

8

There's a brisk business among "credit repair" companies that charge from $50 to more than $1,000 to "fix" your credit report. In many cases, these outfits take your money and do little or nothing to improve your credit report. Often, they just vanish.

So be wary of credit repair companies that guarantee to clean up your credit report. Such promises cannot be kept unless the information in your credit report is actually wrong or out of date.

Remember, too, that if there are genuine mistakes or outdated information in your report, you can fix them yourself. In fact, you can do anything a credit repair company can do—for free or for only a few dollars.

WHAT TO DO IF YOU'RE A VICTIM OF CREDIT REPAIR FRAUD

Has your state passed a law regulating credit repair companies? This may help if you have lost money to a credit repair scam.

Even if your state has no such law, you still may have legal rights that will allow you to take action against the

67

company. Report your problem to your state attorney general's office and local consumer protection agency. While the FTC does not handle individual cases, it can act when it sees a pattern of possible law violations develop. If you have a problem with a credit repair company, write: Credit Practices Division, FTC, Washington, DC 20580.

FOR MORE INFORMATION

The FTC enforces several federal laws involving consumer credit. These include the Equal Credit Opportunity Act, the Fair Credit Billing Act and the Fair Debt Collection Practices Act. For single free copies of brochures about these laws or related publications entitled *Building a Better Credit Record*, *Women and Credit Histories*, *Credit Billing Errors* or *Solving Credit Problems*, write: Public Reference, FTC, Washington, DC 20580.

BATTLING THE BUREAUCRATS

In 1989, I filed a lawsuit against TRW in municipal court, claiming that it had violated my rights by refusing to respond to my requests to remove a CHECKPOINT (fraud indicator) from my credit report. I alleged that TRW's reporting of inaccurate information had caused me severe hardship and damages resulting from the denial of credit.

Subsequently, hundreds of lawsuits were filed against the major credit bureaus throughout the country. Attorney Michael Hsu developed a course entitled "Erasing Bad Credit Through Small Claims Court" and began promoting it in his lectures throughout the country.

On June 6, 1991, consumers urged Congress to rewrite the law governing credit reporting agencies.

Faced with angry consumers in 18 states including California, Equifax, Inc., agreed to overhaul its credit reporting practices. While not formally admitting to any wrongdoing, Equifax agreed to pay $150,000 to the 18 states to cover investigative costs. The firm also agreed to provide consumers with clearly written copies of credit reports for $8 apiece—and free of charge within 60 days of their being rejected for credit. Equifax agreed to improve its credit information gathering and reporting systems to prevent the mixing of one person's file with that of another person.

In December 1991, TRW settled a lawsuit with 19 states and the FIFC. The agreement required TRW to make sweeping changes in its credit reporting business, including providing reports within four days to consumers who ask for them. TRW announced that beginning in 1992, consumers could order complimentary copies of their credit reports once each calendar year. The effective date for the complimentary credit report was April 30, 1992.

In announcing this offer, D. Van Skilling, executive vice president and general manager of TRW Information Systems and Services, said, "Credit reporting must become a true partnership among the consumer, credit grantor and the credit reporting industry." The complimentary credit report will encourage this partnership. TRW is unique among the three national credit reporting companies in offering consumers a complimentary credit report on request each year.

Shirley Rooker, president of Call for Action, an international consumer hotline, said, "TRW's complimentary credit report is an asset consumers should use as part of their financial planning. Because the credit report is updated regularly, a consumer considering a major credit purchase, such as a house or car, may want to request the complimentary report six to eight weeks prior to the planned purchase to assure the information in the report is current. This is a valuable tool and it should not be used frivolously."

To take advantage of this offer, consumers must make their requests in writing on plain paper or personal stationery. To protect consumer privacy, the request should include a document that links the name of the consumer requesting the report with the address the report should be mailed to, such as a photocopy of a billing statement or a driver's license. Telephone requests will not be accepted. TRW also will not accept requests from third parties, such as credit repair clinics writing on behalf of consumers. Consumers should address their requests for a complimentary credit report to:

TRW Complimentary Report
P.O. Box 2350
Chatsworth, CA 91313-2350

This is the only TRW address to use for this.

Consumers must include the following information when writing to request a complimentary report:

- Full name, including middle initial and generation such as Jr., Sr., II or III.
- Current address including zip code.
- Previous addresses including zip code if the consumer has moved in the last five years.
- Social Security number.
- Year of birth.

- Spouse's first name, if married.

- Photocopy of a billing statement, utility bill, driver's license or other document that links the name of the consumer requesting the report with the address the report should be mailed to. This verification is necessary to protect the security of consumers' personal information.

Consumers who fail to include all of this information will be notified that their requests cannot be processed. Otherwise, they should allow approximately two to three weeks for delivery. The credit report will include instructions on how to contact TRW or a local credit bureau with any further questions about the information in the report.

Consumers who want to obtain subsequent copies of their TRW credit reports can do so for a $7.50 fee plus applicable state sales tax (reports are $2 for consumers residing in Maine and $5 for residents of Maryland). By law, consumers are entitled to a free report if they have been denied credit within the past 30 days. TRW's practice is to provide consumers who have been denied credit free reports upon request within 60 days of credit denial.

CREDIT REPORTING AGENCIES COUNTER THE CREDIT CLINICS

9

The conference room was filled with TRW executives. Each one listened intently as Jack from the operational auditing department methodically outlined a detailed plan for extermination of one of the most significant viruses to hit TRW in a very long time. "They are attacking the integrity of our file," Jack said as he threw up another slide. Every head nodded in agreement as Jack completed the professional 45-minute presentation on credit clinics.

The plan seemed simple enough. Tear down their credibility; then they won't have any clients and they'll have to go out of business. Operational auditing was to ensure that each consumer relations department was following company procedures right down to the crossing of every "t" and the dotting of each "i." Public affairs was to strategically plant numerous news articles concerning consumer ripoffs, and the legislative affairs department was to spend about 40 hours developing the basis for legislation prohibiting credit clinic activity.

The Equal Credit Opportunity Act requires creditors to maintain accurate written records for a period of at least 25 months. Storage is expensive, and oftentimes creditors will purge hard data that has aged beyond the minimum requirement. Section 611 of the Fair Credit

Reporting Act is designed as a self-help mechanism for consumers to correct credit reports containing information that is erroneous and misleading or can no longer be verified. The 1971 federal law, which requires credit bureaus to reinvestigate disputed information, has been called a "loophole" by credit executives. In an attempt to close the loophole, TRW successfully lobbied for the Credit Services Act of 1984, a California law requiring credit service companies to adhere to a minimal set of ethical standards for the protection of the customer. A majority of states have enacted similar laws.

Credit clinics, as they were first called, sprang up in Southern California. Entrepreneurs like Michael Hsu and Ken Yarbrough charted the course between the credit bureau and the consumer. Get-rich-quick schemers then entered the picture and muddied the water so much that, for a time, things were quite confusing. Nearly 50 press releases found their way into major newspapers and magazines throughout the country. Each article pointed toward consumer fraud. Detailed horror stories about how consumers were ripped off by a swindler posing as a credit consultant were submitted strategically to the news media.

In the spring of 1989, representatives of various state attorney general's offices, the Federal Trade Commission, the Federal Bureau of Investigation, the U.S. Secret Service, the U.S. Postal Inspectors and local district attorneys' offices created a secret task force to actively investigate the activities of selected credit repair companies throughout the country.

Pressure was applied by the three major credit bureaus: TRW, Trans Union and Equifax. Strategic press releases were channeled through the nonprofit organization Consumer Credit Counseling Service for distribution to the news media. The Better Business Bureau was also coaxed into action.

On July 19, 1989, the Better Business Bureau issued a press release that warned consumers to stay away from all credit repair companies. The release stated that these companies perform absolutely no valuable service to the consumer whatsoever.

Consider the tone of the following release from the National Center for Financial Education dated June 1990:

> *Along with the proliferation of charge cards and the wide availability of credit are many various businesses and organizations dedicated to collecting and reporting (to merchants and others who will pay for it) data on an individual's credit and debt repayment history. In the course of this activity, now highly automated with a nationwide network of reporting offices and well over 150 million credit files, incorrect or incomplete information can get into a credit file.*

It soon became apparent that this business of reporting credit history could stand a little fairness, and Congress enacted The Fair Credit Reporting Act in April 1971. This act established guidelines for credit bureaus, credit reporting agencies and creditors to follow in reporting on an individual's credit history in addition to giving consumers certain rights. It included a procedure by which people can obtain a copy of their credit report. Also, a method was established to enable and help people have the information verified and make necessary changes, additions and deletions to their credit report.

In the 1980s, a credit repair industry emerged. People in all parts of the country have paid out hundreds of thousands of dollars to these firms with little or nothing to show for it. Over half of these firms advertising in the yellow pages are out of business. Three bills are now pending before Congress to regulate these firms.

The following is a letter from Trans Union to members of the Merchants Association:

March 1, 1989

TO: Members of Merchants Association

The integrity of credit history information is under attack by credit clinics throughout the country. No doubt you have seen the advertisements guaranteeing "to erase bad credit" and have wondered how it can be done. Bad credit can only be erased if you, the credit grantor, allow it to be done.

Credit clinics advise consumers to challenge the accuracy of every adverse item of information in the file in the hope that you, the credit grantor, will not respond to a reverification request within a reasonable period of time. Failure to respond forces the credit bureau to delete the adverse item in compliance with the Fair Credit Reporting Act. When this happens, the credit clinic wins. Good customers and other credit grantors are the losers.

Another credit clinic scheme is to "negotiate" payment of the adverse account with the credit grantor in return for a "favorable report" or "no rating" to the credit bureau. This form of blackmail also undermines the integrity of the credit information and makes a winner out of the credit clinic.

We are confident that you support and depend on accurate credit history information. The enclosed statement on integrity of credit information has the approval and support of the national Credit Grantor Advisory Group sponsored by our trade association, Associated Credit Bureaus, Inc. Please indicate your support by completing and returning the attached policy statement.

Finally, please take a moment to ask your credit department how it is processing requests for reverification of adverse information from the credit bureau. Also, have contacts been received requesting the removal of adverse information if an account is paid in full? On the reverse side of this letter is the verification form that we use to confirm information in our file. If you learn that you are inadvertently contributing to the success of the credit clinics, please instruct your personnel on the proper handling of these requests. Together we will assure the continued integrity of the credit file.

Sincerely,

Larry D. Wages
General Manager (Trans Union)

POLICY STATEMENT ON INTEGRITY OF CREDIT INFORMATION

Recognizing that the integrity and effective functioning of the consumer credit system is dependent upon the furnishing, maintaining and reporting of factual credit history information, which is a responsibility shared by credit grantors and consumer reporting agencies alike, our company reaffirms:

1. *That consumer credit history information will be reported in a factual, precise and objective manner.*

2. *That requests by consumers for reverification of challenged information will be processed promptly.*

3. *That upon the request of a consumer, we will promptly review that consumer's account, disclosing to the consumer the factual payment record as reported to consumer reporting agencies and/or to other creditors.*

4. *That unless an error is discovered, the consumer will be advised that the factual credit history information will continue to be reported.*

Here is a response to that letter, written by Ken Yarbrough, executive director of the Consumer Credit Commission. The (now-defunct) Commission was founded by Yarbrough in 1988 as a consumer rights organization designed to head off abuses by the credit reporting agencies. Yarbrough, the former chief of computer security for TRW, makes the case that consumers have a legitimate right to negotiate settlements with creditors in exchange for updated remarks on their credit reports. (For more details on the specifics of this technique, refer to my previous book, *Life After Debt*.)

Consumer Credit Commission
4286 Redwood Highway, #350
San Rafael, CA 94903

On March 17, 1989, a request was received to initiate a staff opinion relevant to the Trans Union letter placed on the reverse side of this document. Pursuant to that request, the following findings are hereby presented:

The Commission has found no evidence which indicates that factual credit history information is under attack by credit clinics throughout the country. Nor has the Commission found substantiating evidence indicating that the credit grantor is negligent in his duties, as indicated.

Additionally, the Commission is not aware of conditions whereby the "credit clinic wins" or where "good customers and other credit grantors are the losers." The law in this regard is exact. Information (either positive or negative) which is found to be inaccurate or can no longer be verified must be promptly deleted from the file. The deletion of non-verifiable information, either negative or positive, is an asset to the credit community and the consumer to whom it relates, and it is in direct compliance with the law.

Negotiation of contractual items is a basic principle of business. The Commission is of the staff opinion that negotiated items are not a form of "blackmail" as indicated in the letter. Further, the Commission supports the basic rights of individuals and business firms when related to compromised agreement. The Commission is aware of a $3.2 million judgment recently awarded a consumer against a major bank. Effective negotiations early in this event may very well have resulted in a favorable settlement, in that the actual dollar damage amounted to only $2,000.

America's entire judicial system supports the usage of the negotiated settlement and compromised agreement. Numerous lawsuits have been halted or avoided entirely through negotiated settlements. States have enacted legislation which favors compromised agreements, and many industries routinely depend upon negotiation as their primary means of conducting business.

Traffic schools educate infraction violators relevant to traffic safety. Upon completion (as a negotiated settlement), adverse traffic history is promptly deleted from the offender's official record. The Commission thus supports the use of negotiation and compromised agreement between the creditor and consumer.

The Commission does not visualize the making of a "winner" of a credit clinic simply because the credit grantor agrees to a negotiated settlement. The integrity and effective functioning of the consumer credit system is:

1. *Creation of a consumer reporting agency which integrates and fully verifies information received from credit bureaus, credit grantors and the consumer to whom it relates; and provides a certified consumer report.*

2. *Credit grantor education as it relates to creditworthiness and interpretations of consumer reports.*

3. *Detailed education programs concerning consumer budgeting procedures, long-term, intermediate and immediate financial goals, and consumer credit rights.*

4. *The production of a detailed consumer financial plan to include a strategy for savings, investments and charity, as well as a strategy for the acquisition of major purchases that must be financed, such as automobiles, real estate and so on.*

It is in this regard that the Commission recommends against the adoption of a policy which limits opportunities for compromise between consumers and credit grantors, and finds that these situations are better handled on a case-by-case basis.

Respectfully submitted,

Ken Yarbrough
Executive Director

TRW and Trans Union have also been putting the pressure on the small independent credit bureaus. They put several of these small bureaus out of business completely when it was learned that credit reports had been supplied to credit repair agencies. On one occasion, an agency was told that it could not order any more credit reports from a particular bureau until it signed the following agreement:

I_____am affiliated with _____. I/We are not a "credit clean-up" service. I also understand that my membership fee is nonrefundable.

DATE:
Signature:
DATE:
Signature:
Credit Bureau Manager

Repair Your Own Credit

According to Jayson Orvis, Senior Paralegal with The Law Offices for Consumer Affairs, "The credit bureaus have unitedly declared war against the credit repair companies and those selling instruction on how to do-it-yourself. The bureaus lambaste credit repair companies in the media and send anti-credit repair literature to anyone they suspect of using credit repair services."

Recently, a couple who was using the services of a credit repair company received a scathing letter of reproach from their local credit bureau. The letter chastened them for relying on the "unethical" methods of credit repair and forcefully pointed out, "your credit remains unchanged." The couple was amused and bewildered as almost all of their many negative credit listings, including a bankruptcy, had been deleted.

U.S. District Court Judge J. Wexler entered the following legal opinion in the Federal Supplement: "Since allowing third parties to assist consumers will likely lead to the expedited correction of credit reports, it will further the purchases of the Fair Credit Reporting Act."

Despite the propaganda to the contrary, you can repair your own credit. Having worked directly with individuals on both sides of the credit repair fence, I have concluded that every type of credit problem can be resolved with the right combination of patience, effort and the proper application of the law.

Unfortunately, the majority of so called "credit clinics" do little, if anything, to improve their client's credit reports. Credit repair companies cannot do anything for you that you cannot do for yourself. More importantly, the money you spend on a credit repair company could be better spent paying off your bills and correcting your credit problems yourself.

Q: Are all credit repair companies ripoffs?

A: No. Some companies make an effort to help consumers correct mistakes on their credit reports and assist them in understanding credit reports. They also may provide assistance to people who are uncomfortable about contacting credit reporting agencies or negotiating with creditors.

However, many credit repair companies misrepresent what they can do by claiming to have the ability to remove all negative information from credit reports. Credit repair companies describe this process as "secret," but they don't do anything that you cannot do for yourself. Many credit repair firms have gone out of business after taking hundreds of dollars from individuals and doing nothing for them.

Q: How do credit repair companies "erase bad credit?"

A: The main way credit repair companies operate is that they bombard credit reporting agencies with requests to verify information. If a credit reporting agency cannot verify an entry, it will remove the information from the report. However, once the information is verified, it will go back in the report.

Q: What about companies that offer a guarantee?

A: Credit repair companies often claim they can "guarantee" to get you a credit card, regardless of your credit history. In fact, these companies do not always honor their guarantees.

In some cases, what you get is a "secured" bank credit card. (A secured credit card is a Visa or MasterCard that requires the cardholder to maintain a savings account equal to or double the credit line.) These cards often have high fees; it may cost you $100 to $200 just to get the card. In other cases, you get a card that only allows you to buy items in a catalog from a business that you probably never heard of.

Sometimes, these credit repair firms will just take your money and run—you will not get any credit, regardless of what they promised.

Q: Isn't credit repair fraudulent?

A: Some companies try to get people credit by having them apply using personal financial information of people with good credit histories. It is a criminal act to apply for credit under someone else's name. Do not do business with one of these companies! You can, however, legally dispute inaccurate information on your credit reports, according to the Fair Credit Reporting Act.

Q: How can I find a legitimate credit service agency?

A: Before doing business with a company, contact the Better Business Bureau in your area and find out if there have been complaints about the company in the past. Also check with your local district attorney or consumer affairs office to see if the company is under investigation. Ask the credit repair company to show you a copy of its bond and business license. If the company hesitates, take your business elsewhere.

The North American Consumer Alliance (NACA) is a nonprofit consumer advocacy group that offers its members referrals to attorneys specializing in credit law. Call 1-800-497-NACA for more information. Other strategies, such as mortgage acceleration and rapid debt reduction are covered in my previous book, *Life After Debt*.

You may also be able to get free or low-cost help through Consumer Credit Counseling Service, a nonprofit organization with offices in most major cities in the U.S. This service assists consumers who have problems paying their bills (but are not yet in collection). They work out flexible payment plans to make debt repayment more feasible. Check your local phone directory or call 1-800-388-CCCS.

Q: What advice would you give to someone who is thinking about starting a credit repair company?

A: Start by reading everything you can find on the subject of consumer credit. Then get your own house in order first. Clean up your own bad credit before trying to help someone else. Then offer your services for free to a few selected friends and family members. Find out what it's really like to negotiate with creditors and deal with credit reporting agencies. If, after having done all that, you still want to become a credit consultant, check out all the laws in your area by contacting your state department of consumer affairs and your local district attorney's office. Obtain a business license, post the required bond and hang out your shingle. It is also important to make sure your contracts follow the guidelines of the law by including the required cancellation notices and other notifications as mentioned earlier in this book.

Personally, I would suggest working under the umbrella of an attorney's office, a real estate broker or a nonprofit agency. This would exempt you from the Credit Services Act and similar laws governing credit repair companies.

I would also suggest that you consider working as a consumer mediator under the Alternative Dispute Resolution legislation in your state. Or, even better, start your own credit reporting agency. Contact Associated Credit Bureaus, Inc., 1090 Vermont Avenue NW, Suite 200, Washington, D.C. 20005-4905 for more information.

Q: What do I do if I have a complaint against a credit repair company?

A: First, ask the company to return your money in full. If it refuses, write a letter threatening to sue the company in small claims court and report it to the Better Business Bureau, local district attorney's office, state attorney general, department of consumer affairs and the FTC. Keep a copy of all contracts and correspondence for your files, and send them to the appropriate agencies when you file your small claims suit and formal complaints.

THE IMPORTANCE OF GOOD CREDIT

11

*"Credit is the ability to pay later
for debts incurred today."*

A person with "good credit" manages credit well and pays bills on time. Good credit and a healthy credit rating are more important now than in past years. Here's why:

- Today, you need good credit to get more credit. If you want to buy a house or a car, or get a credit card, the bank or credit union will check your credit report. An insurance company will check your report if you apply for more insurance.

- Good credit is convenient. Many businesses strongly prefer the use of credit cards. It's very difficult to rent a car without a credit card. It's sometimes hard to rent a hotel room without one. Businesses prefer "plastic money" for different reasons—one reason is their own convenience. However, because of these policies, most people should probably consider obtaining at least one credit card. (If you do not handle credit well, you may not want to get one. A credit card is useful, but may make matters worse for some people.)

87

- More and more employers are checking the credit ratings of prospective employees. Not all employers do. However, those that do check look unfavorably on a negative credit rating.

- Available credit is helpful for unplanned situations and emergencies: Having good credit does not mean being in debt! Rather, it means having the unused capacity to obtain credit. Credit capacity is useful for convenience, emergencies and unplanned bills. You may have a regular income and always pay your bills on time. Unfortunately, this doesn't equal a good credit rating.

You may be denied credit because of "insufficient credit history." That means, your lifetime of bill payments is not recorded in the computers that make up today's credit system. You may have paid your bills on a "cash basis," instead of with credit cards. Or, your credit may have been with local banks, credit unions and department stores. These local businesses may not report monthly mortgage or loan payments to credit bureaus. So, even though you've used credit all your life, you could apply for new credit and find that your credit report is blank. This lack of credit history can hurt your application.

You may be denied credit because your credit report is mixed up with someone else's. Your personal credit history may be on your credit report and reflect positively, but your credit report may list the bad parts of someone else's credit history, too.

You may be denied credit simply because of your age, race or marital status. According to the Equal Credit Opportunities Act, it is illegal to discriminate on the basis of age, race or marital status, but it does sometimes happen. Many divorced and widowed women report special credit problems. When they were married, their credit was in their spouses' names, not their own. Their credit history is a blank.

Finally, some banks or other lenders may illegally discount nonsalary income. The Equal Credit Opportunities Act requires creditors who consider income to consider sources of income, including Social Security, child support and alimony equally with employment income.

CAUSES OF POOR CREDIT

If you're like most adult American consumers, you probably have at least one negative item on your credit report. In some cases, these negative items are inaccurate or misleading. Such inaccuracies can be caused by clerical errors, mistaken identities or fraud. In some cases you may find accounts that you believe to have been paid or current, reflecting an unpaid or delinquent status. In other cases, you may find accounts or other information that belong to someone else with a similar name. This is common with Juniors and Seniors in the same household. Most of the time, however, the information found on your credit reports will reflect your payment history for various accounts over the last several years. In light of the rising divorce rate, recent recession and problems with the health care insurance system, many individuals have found themselves unable to make ends meet at one time or another. Many of us have suffered medical problems, job layoffs or other temporary setbacks that caused us to fall behind on our bills for a period of time. Unfortunately, such setbacks may continue to haunt us for years to come in the form of negative information on our credit reports.

Another major cause of poor credit is poor judgement. Many consumers overextend themselves with credit cards, signature loans, high car payments, second mortgages and overdraft checking privileges. Before they know it, they are over their heads in debt and unable to make all of their payments. In the most extreme cases, individuals have found themselves in bankruptcy court, small claims court, or facing foreclosure. These "public record" items can be even more damaging to a credit rating.

Some of us are simply poor money managers. In spite of having more than enough income to cover monthly expenses, many individuals simply "forget" to pay all of their bills on time, or neglect to mail them before the due date. As a result their credit reports are littered with late payments, delinquencies and collection accounts.

Many people today are faced with personal financial problems. And things can look bleak when you're burdened with bills that add up to more than you earn each month. The reasons for financial problems are, of course, as various as the people who experience them. A loss or reduction in income. A change in marital status. Unexpected or emergency expenses. And then there's the ready availability of credit itself. Credit can be so convenient that it's tempting to use too much of it.

Whether it's the result of inaccurate information in your files or poor decisions in the past, a negative credit rating can cause you much hardship and humiliation.

Now you can begin to take the necessary action toward repairing your own credit. In the next chapter you will learn a simple step-by-step approach to reestablishing your credit—regardless of your present situation.

SEVEN STEPS TO RE-ESTABLISHING YOUR CREDIT

12

Your creditworthiness influences not only whether you can obtain a loan or purchase goods and services on credit, but may also affect employment, living accommodations or obtaining insurance. If you have a poor credit history, it will take time for you to regain your credibility with credit grantors. You must be able to show that in spite of previous debt problems, you can now handle credit in a financially responsible manner. To assist in this process, here are six steps you can follow.

STEP ONE: PAY OFF YOUR DEBTS

Develop a liquidation plan to repay your debts. Determine how much you can repay each month until you have paid off what you owe. Then, pay your bills on time. Lenders generally look more favorably on individuals who have solved debt problems than those who ignore them. It will help to restore your credit if you can bring your debt balance to zero. If you would like help in budgeting or assistance in developing a realistic repayment schedule, you may wish to contact a Consumer Credit Counseling Service office. To find the office closest to you, call its referral number at 1-800-388-CCCS.

Another alternative is the North American Consumer Alliance. It can provide you with referrals to attorneys specializing in debt reorganization and negotiated settlement. This group has been highly successful in helping consumers avoid bankruptcy and settle accounts with the IRS and student loan administration. Call 1-800-497-NACA.

STEP TWO: DESIGN A PLAN TO MANAGE YOUR MONEY

Often people develop financial problems because they overextend their credit use. In order to reduce the likelihood that you will find yourself in a credit crunch again and help you reduce debt, analyze your spending habits, create financial goals and set spending priorities. You have now begun to take control of your finances.

STEP THREE: PAY WITH CASH

Even if you have some credit available, you are more likely to change your spending habits by not using it. When you pay with cash or even a check, it forces you to recognize that the money you can spend is limited to the amount of funds you have in your checking account. Banks have begun to issue debit cards, which also serve this purpose since the amount you spend is immediately deducted from your account. You will need to make choices about what you can afford to buy and, therefore, you will have to determine your priorities.

STEP FOUR: OBTAIN YOUR CREDIT REPORT

Most credit bureaus are part of one of the "Big Three" automated reporting systems: TRW, Equifax or Trans Union. After you have been denied credit because of negative information, you may obtain a free copy of your credit report from the bureau that supplied the information. The bureaus will allow you up to 60 days to make this request. While TRW will provide you with a free credit report yearly, there is a charge for obtaining your report through Equifax or Trans Union. However, since each report is different, you should check your credit history in all three systems. If you believe that there is an error in your file, you can write the credit bureau and fill out a dispute form. The bureau will verify the information with the creditor to insure that it is correct. If the creditor states it is accurate, and after you write the creditor there is still a disagreement, you may submit a written statement in less than 100 words explaining the dispute to the credit bureau, and it will become part of your record.

STEP FIVE: APPLY FOR SECURED CREDIT

There are several alternatives for obtaining secured credit. Credit is secured when something of value is pledged to assure loan repayment. One place to start to gain secured credit is access to credit cardholder privileges through your parents or spouse. You may also have a relative or friend who will co-sign a loan.

Another option is providing an "enhanced down payment" which might be as much as 50 percent of the purchase price. If you do not have telephone, gas or electricity service in your name, you may try to open accounts with these utility companies. By providing a security deposit, you may be able to obtain this form of credit.

If you have a savings account at a bank or credit union, you may be able to obtain a signature loan; that is, borrow a small amount using the savings account as collateral. Some banks will issue you a secured credit card. When

93

you put a deposit in the bank and obtain a credit line equal to or one and a half times a percentage of your deposit, the deposit acts as collateral from which the bank can draw if you do not pay on time; in effect, securing the card. However, remember that in addition, as with any credit application, you often will be required to have a minimum salary and minimum length of residence to be accepted for secured credit.

In the past couple of years, major banks and companies such as Chase Manhattan, Citibank, Montgomery Ward, Signet Bank and Western Union have all launched secured cards. Interest rates on secured cards, which used to be 21 percent and higher, are falling; some are now as low as their unsecured counterparts. An example: Federal Savings Bank of Rogers, Ark., 1-800-290-9060, is offering a secured card with a rate of 8 percent, and a $55 annual fee. Interest is charged from the day the purchase is posted.

First Consumers National Bank, 1-800-876-3262, offers a secured MasterCard with a $300 minimum deposit and a credit limit of 150 percent of the savings deposit. Signet Bank, 1-800-333-7116, will approve applicants with prior bankruptcy. The $300 minimum deposit earns 5 percent interest and there is a 25-day grace period. MasterCard, 1-800-710-6000, can provide a free list of banks that offer secured MasterCard.

STEP SIX: APPLY FOR UNSECURED CREDIT

A local department store may be more likely to issue you a charge card than a national creditor. If you can offer a reasonable explanation for your past credit behavior and show that you are now financially responsible, this information will generally help. Once you obtain a charge card and pay your bills promptly for a reasonable length of time, your credit line will probably be increased.

However, if you cannot get a department store card, you can begin by purchasing an item on the layaway plan. When you show that you are a reliable customer, the store will be more inclined to provide you with a charge card. Finally, you do not want to try more than a few stores to obtain credit because creditor inquiries will appear on your credit report. Too many inquiries may cause creditors to think you are applying for more credit than you can afford and they may reject your application.

STEP SEVEN: CONTINUE TO EDUCATE YOURSELF

The credit system is extremely intricate and constantly changing. Every year, millions of Americans are caught up in a web of overwhelming debt and confusion. The rising level of personal debt, coupled with the introduction of dozens of new products in the credit marketplace, makes the need for timely, complete and user-friendly consumer education greater than ever.

Read as many books as you can find on the subject of consumer credit and personal finance. Attend seminars and subscribe to newsletters. To save money, visit your local library. Your increased awareness of the system will help you to guard against repeating the same mistakes in the future. As you continue to educate yourself, you will also increase your confidence in your own ability to become master of your own financial destiny. Remember, debt is slavery.

These simple steps, when diligently put into action, will dramatically improve your credit status—regardless of your present situation. The important thing is to begin now by putting these ideas into practice in your daily life.

For additional information or assistance, refer to the publications and resources listed in the back of this book.

CHANGING OR CORRECTING YOUR CREDIT REPORT

13

Q: Can negative information be removed from your credit report?

A: Yes, if the information is incorrect or outdated. The law says that if negative information is correct, it can remain for up to seven years. Bankruptcy can remain for up to 10 years.

Q: If negative information can't be removed, what can I do?

A: The law gives consumers the right to add a 100-word statement of dispute to their credit file. This offers the chance to explain negative items.

Q: How can errors and omissions be corrected?

A: A consumer has the right to request an investigation of any information that is incomplete, incorrect and out of date. These requests must be in writing (the credit bureau will send you a dispute form along with your credit report, or you can use the "Letter of Dispute" on page 103). The agency must then investigate and verify the information. If the information is not verified within a reasonable time period (30 days), it may be removed by reason of doubt. However, if the information was correct it can be put back on your report at a later time. If the information is found to be incorrect, it must be removed.

Q: How will the credit bureau respond?

A: The credit reporting agency may respond with one of the following answers to your dispute:

- We have changed your credit file as requested.

- Your credit file will not be changed because

  _____.

- The party(s) involved did not respond, so the information is being removed by reason of default.

Q: What if the response is no change to the report?

A: You have the right to request that the information be reinvestigated or you can place a 100-word statement of dispute in your report.

Q: How do I read my credit report?

A: Your credit report will include a listing of various codes and abbreviations along with an explanation to help you understand what it says about your payment history. For example, accounts are usually listed as O (open), I (installment) or R (revolving). A number from 0 to 9 will rate the account as to how promptly the account has been paid. A "0" indicates the account is too new to rate, a "1" indicates the account is current or paid as agreed, a "9" indicates an account that was written off as a bad debt or "charge off." Thus, an account listed as "R 9" means a revolving charge account that was "charged off" as a bad debt.

Q: How is bankruptcy reported to the credit bureaus?

A: Bankruptcy will show up on your credit report as a public record and may remain on your report for up to 10 years. Each account included in the bankruptcy will show up on your credit report as either "charge off" or "bankruptcy liquidation."

Q: Are there any positive items that can show up on a credit report?

A: Other than your identifying information, such as name, address, etc., the only positive remarks on a credit report will be for accounts that are either "paid satisfactorily" or "current account with no late payments." Nonrated items may include inquiries, accounts closed by consumer request or refinance. Other items on a credit report are usually negative, such as late payments, collection accounts, charge offs, tax liens, repossessions, foreclosure, etc.

Q: How can public record items be removed from a credit report?

A: If the item is incorrect, misleading or obsolete it can be disputed. If the bureau cannot verify the disputed information, it must be deleted from your credit report. If a lien or judgment has already been paid, but the report reflects it as being unpaid, you should contact the original creditor and request a discharge form. That discharge form is then submitted to the court clerk to be recorded, and a copy of the recorded document sent to the credit bureau as evidence that the lien or judgment has been satisfied.

Q: Do consumers have the right to ask that their accounts not be sent for collection?

A: Yes. If you are late in paying on your account, you should contact the creditor and ask to make an alternative payment plan. In some cases, you may be able to make reduced monthly payments or "skip" a payment without being penalized. In other cases (such as with an account that has already been charged off) you may be able to negotiate a settlement payment with the creditor. This strategy is covered in great detail in my previous book, *Life After Debt*.

TRACKING YOUR DISPUTES

It is important to organize and maintain copies of all of your correspondence with the credit bureaus and individual creditors. One way to do this is to use separate file folders for each of the three credit bureaus, and a separate folder for correspondence with creditors and collection agencies. Staple a sheet of lined paper inside each file folder to keep track of telephone conversations and time lines. Some of your contacts may require specific follow-up action. Therefore, it is important to make specific and accurate notes. When you contact a bureau, credit grantor or collection agency, record and summarize that contact on the sheet of paper in the appropriate file folder. Use a calendar book to make note of follow-up dates or appointments.

SAMPLE STATEMENTS OF DISPUTE

Under the Fair Credit Reporting Act you have the right to add to your credit report a statement of up to 100 words regarding any item(s) you wish to clarify. This statement will then appear on all subsequent reports sent to your credit grantors. Here are some examples:

- *"This is not my account. I have never owed money to this creditor. Apparently, a mistake was made in the reporting."*

- *"On (date), I moved to another address. I notified all creditors, including (name of creditor) promptly. (Name of creditor) was slow in changing my address in its file. Subsequently, I did not receive my billing statement for (how long). Once I received the statement at my new address, I paid this creditor."*

- *"On (date), I was hospitalized at (facility). The medical bills were forwarded to my insurance company for payment. My insurance company delayed in paying and the hospital turned my account over for collection. Afterwards, my insurance company paid the hospital bill in full. The hospital's collection agency refused, however, to change the negative rating of my account."*

- *"This account belongs to my former spouse. My name is no longer on this account."*

- *"On (date), I ordered merchandise from (name of company) on my account. The merchandise was defective and I returned it to the sender. The company continued to send me a bill for the returned defective merchandise. The company went out of business before I was able to have my account properly credited."*

SAMPLE CREDIT REPORT REQUEST

Date: _____
To: Credit Bureau
Please send me a copy of my credit report.

My full name is: _____
                           (Jr/Sr/etc.)

My Social Security number is: _____

My date of birth is: _____

My address is: _____

Previous address (last five years): _____

_____

    I may have received credit in the last five years under the following names (e.g. maiden name, etc.): _____

_____

_____

    Enclosed is a copy of a recent billing statement (or driver's license) as proof of my name and address.

    ____ (If applicable) I am making this request for a free credit report since I have been denied credit in the last 60 days based on one of your reports. A copy of the denial letter is attached for your information.

    ___ A check or money order for $8 is enclosed.*

Sincerely,

    * This fee pertains to credit reports if you have not been denied credit within the last 60 days or if you request an additional report from TRW within the same calendar year.

SAMPLE LETTER OF DISPUTE

Date:_____

To: (Name of agency)_____

ATTN: Consumer Relations

RE: Name:_____

ID#:____ Address:_____

Telephone:_____

Social Security number:_____

Date of birth:_____

Please begin an investigation of the following items listed on my credit report that do not belong in my credit file.

Company's name	Account	Reason for dispute
_____	_____	_____
_____	_____	_____
_____	_____	_____
_____	_____	_____
_____	_____	_____
_____	_____	_____

Please update my credit report and send me a copy at the conclusion of your investigation. Send the results to the following organizations that have reviewed my credit report in the past six months and/or to employers that have reviewed it during the past two years.

Thank you for your help and prompt attention in this matter.

Respectfully,

(your name)

THE ETHICS OF
CREDIT IMPROVEMENT

14

Since the publication of Life After Debt, I have received hundreds of letters from consumers requesting information on the ethics of disputing accurate credit information. As I have clearly described in my previous books, there are certainly a number of legal ways in which accurate information can be removed from your credit reports. The question remains, is it ethical?

The following article by Jayson Orvis is reprinted with permission from "Inside Angle," the newsletter of the North American Consumer Alliance (NACA). I believe it addresses this important issue.

"Credit Repair" has not been kind to the American consumer. In fact, the phrase is synonymous with fraud. This is the stigma we face as we offer a membership wherein the client is offered an alternative to "credit prison." Because the nasty reputation of credit repair sometimes washes over into our space, we are often called upon to defend the ethics of our service.

Despite the disrepute which taints credit improvement, our service is clearly analogous to the service provided by a defense attorney. The credit report is no more than an allegation. Unfortunately, most citizens never challenge that allegation. By enlisting the Law Offices through N.A.C.A. to their defense, our clients employ us to enter a plea of "not guilty." We take an affirmative defense; we offer a reasonable alibi and leave it to the bureaus to substantiate their allegation. If the bureau claims to have investigated and affirmed the allegation, we appeal the decision. Eventually, we find that most credit report allegations are at some point untenable and are removed.

Removing record of a negative credit account, which did actually exist, is undoubtedly ethically sound. We belong to a fundamentally capitalistic civilization and the credit bureaus capitalize on consumer information. Unlike our legal system, the bureaus take no oath to truth, equity and the common good. No American has the moral obligation to support any business venture or corporation, much less a corporation which may well destroy their financial life. The information tended by the credit bureaus is ethically "up for grabs."

The credit bureaus would maintain every piece of credit information forever if it weren't for federal law which has directed them to remove most items after seven years. In essence, the credit bureaus themselves practice credit repair, basically at the seven-year mark. If it is right to remove accurate credit accounts after seven years, why would it be wrong to do so in less time?

In relationship to the consumer, the credit bureaus do not concern themselves with the impact of the information. This information often misrepresents the creditworthiness of the consumer. By tagging good citizens as "deadbeats" the bureaus damage the creditors, the economy and, most importantly, the individual. Several policies and techniques employed by the credit bureaus appear most abusive to the American consumer; these we cite as justification of our opposition to the present credit reporting system.

Seven years (10 years for bankruptcy and some court accounts) credit bondage punishes the debtor unjustly. At no point have the credit bureaus ever conducted a study determining seven years to be the point of deadbeat rejuvenation. The seven-year mark is entirely arbitrary. In fact, Dr. Bonnie Guiton, adviser to President Bush on consumer affairs, remarked, "...it is our understanding that computer models that predict creditworthiness find most information that is more than two years old nonessential." Based on experience with our clientele, seven years is truly too long. Within a year or two, most consumers completely recover from an economic crisis. For the remaining five or six years, they are left hobbled—forced to rent homes, pay outrageous interest on high-risk auto loans, forgo the convenience of credit cards and pay cash for every expenditure. By expelling the consumer from the credit loop, the economy suffers. Our clients come to us on the financial upswing. If they can afford our membership, they are most likely on the way back to financial abundance. These are consumers fully recovered from crises, reengaged to financial responsibility and anxious to reenter the credit economy. For them, we offer a deserved parole from the credit prison which they entered as their financial world fell apart.

The credit bureaus have not been able to maintain reasonable accuracy in their credit profiles. The bureaus claim an error ratio under 1 percent. In reality, studies conducted by neutral third parties have determined the credit report error ratio to be closer to 40 percent. Unfortunately for the consumer, the credit bureaus choose to err on the side of negative information. As our clients' files have passed through our offices, we have noticed a high incidence of file mergers—the worst kind of file error. In a file merger, the credit of another person with a similar name is spread onto the file of the innocent bystander.

Oddly, the credit bureaus fiercely resist correction of these obvious errors. We have found the only way to prompt them to revision is through a lawsuit.

Credit reporting makes up only a small portion of the revenue which the bureaus claim each year. The databases really pay off in the sales of information. From generic target marketing lists to invasive personal investigative inquiries, the bureaus cull a pool of information larger than any in the civilized world. The end loser is the consumer who values his privacy. The horror stories keep coming about individuals whose jobs have been lost, insurance canceled, reputation ruined by sloppy collection and dissemination of personal information. This does not include the mass irritation experienced by consumers forced to wade through reams of junk mail. Privacy is a thing of the past—and the blame can be firmly placed on the credit bureaus.

America is not the only country in the world whose economy utilizes consumer credit. Other countries, such as Great Britain, extend credit based on the individual's present credit standing. A grand-scale revision of the credit reporting system in the United States would not throw our credit economy into chaos and distress. Until that day, we should feel comfortable that the removal of negative credit accounts before the seven year mark isn't unpatriotic, it's not unfair and it's not unethical.

For more information, contact:

North American Consumer Alliance
6911 South 1300 East, Suite 500
Midvale, UT 84047
801-263-1373
800-497-NACA

CONCLUSION

C

WHERE TO GET HELP

The various consumer credit laws presented in this book are enforced by federal, state and local agencies. If you would like further information or have a particular problem you would like addressed, you can contact the appropriate agencies.

If your problem is with a credit repair company, credit bureau, debt collector, consumer finance company or retail department store, write to:

Division of Credit Practices
Federal Trade Commission
Washington, DC 20580

State and local consumer protection offices resolve individual consumer complaints, conduct informational and educational programs and enforce consumer protection and fraud laws. Local offices can be particularly helpful for both prepurchase information and complaint handling, because they are often familiar with local businesses and laws. Check your local telephone directory's white pages in the "Government" section for State Attorney

General, Consumer Protection Division or Consumer Affairs Division. Your city attorney or district attorney office's fraud division may also be helpful.

PRIVATE ORGANIZATIONS

The North American Consumer Alliance (NACA) is a nonprofit consumer advocacy group that overcomes its members tax, credit, debt and legal challenges through the engagement of professional legal counsel and the promotion of consumer awareness. Call 1-800-497-NACA or write:

North American Consumer Alliance
6911 South 1300 East, Suite 500
Midvale, UT 84047

The Better Business Bureau assists consumers by investigating disputes with companies and providing consumer mediation and arbitration services. Check your white pages under Better Business Bureau or write to:

Council of Better Business Bureaus, Inc.
4200 Wilson Blvd.
Arlington, VA 22203

The Consumer Credit Counseling Service assists consumers who have problems in paying their bills (but are not yet in collection). Call 1-800-388-CCCS or write to:

National Foundation for Consumer Credit, Inc.
8611 2nd Avenue, Suite 100
Silver Spring, MD 20910

Consumer Action staffs a free complaint/information switchboard from 10:00 a.m. to 3:00 p.m. (PST) on weekdays. It provides nonlegal consumer advice and referrals. Write to:

Consumer Action
116 New Montgomery Street
San Francisco, CA 94105

Consumer Loan Advocates is a nonprofit organization that promotes consumer awareness and publishes "Rip-Off Reviews," a monthly newsletter. Call 708-615-0024 or write:

Consumer Loan Advocates
655 Rockland Road, #106
Lake Bluff, IL 60044

The National Center for Financial Education provides information about credit doctors and credit reporting agencies. Write:

NCFE
P.O. Box 34070
San Diego, CA 92163

Associated Credit Bureaus, Inc., a trade organization, offers a free brochure called "Consumers, Credit Bureaus and The Fair Credit Reporting Act." Write to:

Associated Credit Bureaus, Inc.
1090 Vermont Ave., NW, Suite 200
Washington, DC 20005-4905

THE BIG THREE

The following are the addresses you'll need to request a copy of your credit report. For a complimentary copy of your TRW credit report, write to:

TRW Complimentary Report
P.O. Box 2350
Chatsworth, CA 91313-2350

For other assistance, write to:

TRW Credit Data
National Consumer Relations Center
660 N. Central Expressway, Exit 28
P.O. Box 949
Allen, TX 75002

Equifax Credit Information Services
P.O. Box 740241
Atlanta, GA 30374-0241

Trans Union Credit Information
Consumer Relations Center
P.O. Box 7000
North Olmsted, OH 44070-7000

RESOURCES

R

Credit Secrets: How to Erase Bad Credit
Paladin Press
P.O. Box 1307
Boulder, CO 80306
800-392-2400

Contains a detailed description of the identification systems used by each of the major credit bureaus, along with dynamic strategies for circumventing the system and starting over with a new credit file. Also describes a unique method of "losing" your bankruptcy files and deleting any reference to filing for Chapter 7 or Chapter 13.

How to Beat the Credit Bureaus: The Insider's Guide to Consumer Credit
Paladin Press
P.O. Box 1307
Boulder, CO 80306
800-392-2400

In this intriguing follow-up to his best-selling first book, *Credit Secrets,* author Bob Hammond describes the deceptive web of information systems spun by the powerful corporate credit bureau syndicate and how it is used to victimize, humiliate and defile countless innocent consumers. More importantly, it will show you how to take legal action against an unfair system—and win. Includes documented successful lawsuits against major credit-reporting agencies. This book is must reading for every American consumer.

Life After Debt: How to Repair Your Credit and Get Out of Debt Once and For All
Career Press
180 Fifth Avenue
P.O. Box 34
Hawthorne, NJ 07507
800-CAREER-1

Not a rehash of old information, this book attacks the root causes of indebtedness and teachers consumers how to settle old accounts for pennies on the dollar. You'll also learn how to stop collection agency harassment, billing errors and discrimination. Contains sample letters for reducing monthly payments, credit reporting disputes and negotiated settlement.

ABOUT THE AUTHOR

A

Bob Hammond is one of the nation's leading authorities on consumer credit. He is the author of several books, including *Credit Secrets, How to Beat The Credit Bureaus*, and *Life After Debt*. Hammond has been a guest on hundreds of radio and television talk shows throughout the country. In addition to conducting seminars and lectures on consumer credit and the coming cashless society, he trains real estate and finance industry professionals on how to help their clients get credit approval.

Hammond is an arbitrator for the Better Business Bureau, an investigator for the Fair Housing Council and consultant to Consumer Credit Counseling Services of the Inland Empire. He also works with the North American Consumer Alliance (NACA), a nonprofit consumer advocacy group that helps consumers overcome tax, credit, debt and legal challenges through the engagement of professional legal counsel and the promotion of consumer awareness.

Hammond received his B.A. in psychology and sociology fron the University of the State of New York, Regents College, and he studied screenwriting at the Hollywood Scriptwriting Institute.

Hammond's next book, *Living Debt Free*, will be published by Career Press in the summer of 1995.

INDEX

I

117